BIOLOGY

FOR QUEENSLAND

AN AUSTRALIAN PERSPECTIVE

UNITS

3 & 4

STUDENT WORKBOOK

JESS SAUTNER

SERIES CONSULTANT
ROBYN FLEXMAN

Oxford University Press is a department of the University of Oxford. It furthers the University's objective of excellence in research, scholarship, and education by publishing worldwide. Oxford is a registered trademark of Oxford University Press in the UK and in certain other countries.

Published in Australia by
Oxford University Press
Level 8, 737 Bourke Street, Docklands, Victoria 3008, Australia.

First published 2019
Reprinted 2020

ISBN 9780190320416

Edited by Joy Window
Typeset by Newgen KnowledgeWorks Pvt. Ltd., Chennai, India
Proofread by Jeanette Birtles
Printed in China by Sheck Wah Tong Printing Press Ltd.

CONTENTS

Using *Biology for Queensland An Australian Perspective Units 3 & 4 Student workbook*

Biology for Queensland An Australian Perspective Units 3 & 4 Student workbook is designed to help students succeed in their internal and external assessments. Each activity is supported with an engaging design, full-colour diagrams and answers at the back of the book.

Experiment explorer
Tasks to support the modification of a practical as required in the Student experiment.

Internal assessment support
This workbook includes a practice Data test, Student experiment and Research investigation to help students with their Units 3 & 4 internal assessments.

Data drill
Activities that help students develop the key skills in analysis and interpretation required for the data test.

Research review
Activities that allow students to practise evaluating a claim and identify credible sources for the Research investigation.

Practical manual
Write-in worksheets complement all mandatory and suggested practicals.

Answers
Answers are provided for all chapter activities and practice assessments.

ACKNOWLEDGEMENTS

The author and the publisher wish to thank the following copyright holders for reproduction of their material.

Chapter 1: Newspix/Alison Wynd, 1.4.6; Shutterstock, chapter opener.

Chapter 2: Shutterstock, 2.1, 2.2, chapter opener, table 2a, Unit 3 opener, Unit 3 practice assessment; Alamy/Hind Sight Media, table 2d/ Science Photos, table 2b.

Chapter 3; Alamy/Seaphotoart, chapter opener; Shutterstock, 3.2.

Chapter 4: Alamy/Auscape International Pty Ltd, chapter opener; Shutterstock, 4.2.

Chapter 5: Shutterstock, 5.3, 5.5, chapter opener.

Chapter 6: Getty/Corbis, 6.1; Shutterstock, 6.4, chapter opener, Unit 4 opener, Unit 4 practice assessment opener.

Chapter 7: Shutterstock, 7.1, chapter opener.

Chapter 8: Shutterstock, 8.1, 8.2, chapter opener; Science Photo Library/Look at Sciences, 8.3.

Chapter 9: Shutterstock, 9.1, chapter opener.

Chapter 10: Science Photo Library/Look at Sciences, chapter opener.

Chapter 11: Shutterstock, 11.2, chapter opener.

Chapter 12: Getty/Cultura, chapter opener; Shutterstock, 12.1.

Chapter 13: Shutterstock, 13.1, chapter opener.

Chapter 14: Shutterstock, 14.1, chapter opener.

Chapter 15: Alamy/Eyal Bartov, Unit 4 practice assessment, figure 1/DonSmith, chapter opener; Shutterstock, 15.1 (left), 15.1 (right).

Chapter 16: Alamy/Parmorama, chapter 16 opener; Shutterstock, 16.1.

Every effort has been made to trace the original source of copyright material contained in this book. The publisher will be pleased to hear from copyright holders to rectify any errors or omissions.

Biology toolkit

The Biology Toolkit is a resource for students to refer to while they are working through the activities and practicals in this workbook. It introduces the use of cognitive verbs and provides students with detailed information on how to answer each question. Cognitive verbs are bolded in each activity to highlight them for students.

The three internal assessments are explained in detail in the toolkit, and each has an activity included to practice the skills required for that assessment. The Data test (IA1) is worth 10% of the student's total mark and is completed in Unit 3. The Student experiment (IA2) is worth 20% and is also completed in Unit 3. The Research investigation (IA3) is worth 20% of the student's total mark and is completed in Unit 4.

CHAPTER CHECKLIST

Read this checklist before you complete this chapter's activities and then return to it to check your understanding before your assessments.

Once you have completed this chapter, you can use the 'I can …' statements to assess your understanding of the topics covered by ticking the appropriate box in the 'rating column'.

I can …	Confidently	Partially	Not really
… respond to questions using cognitive verbs			
… explain the requirements of the Unit 3 Data test			
… explain the requirements of the Unit 3 Student experiment			
… explain the requirements of the Unit 4 Research investigation			

1.1 Responding to cognitive verbs

In assessment tasks and examinations, students will encounter **cognitive verbs**. These verbs are 'task words' that will provide information on what is expected in the answer to a question.

It is important to understand the difference between task words. For example, a question that asks a student to 'compare' is different to a command asking a student to 'contrast'. One requires a student to show similarities and differences, while the other is only asking to show the differences.

Understanding exactly what a cognitive verb is asking means that a student can provide exactly what the examiner is looking for. Examiners want to give students marks, but can only do so if the student provides the correct information. For example, if a student **describes** data in their answer, but does not **analyse** the data, they will not receive full marks.

A list of cognitive verbs is provided in the table below and should be referred to when answering questions containing cognitive verbs.

TABLE 1 List of cognitive verbs

Cognitive verb	Definition	Sample question
Analyse	Dissect to ascertain and examine constituent parts and/or their relationships; break down or examine in order to identify the essential elements, features, components or structure; determine the logic and reasonableness of information; examine or consider something in order to explain and interpret it, for the purpose of finding meaning or relationships and identifying patterns, similarities and differences.	**Analyse** the graph provided to identify the relationship between the independent and dependent variables.
Apply	Use knowledge and understanding in response to a given situation or circumstance; carry out or use a procedure in a given or particular situation.	**Apply** your knowledge of photosynthesis to explain how algae receive their energy.
Calculate	Determine or find (e.g. a number, an answer) by using mathematical processes; obtain a numerical answer showing the relevant stages in the working; determine from given facts, figures or information.	**Calculate** the mean for the following dataset.
Compare	Display recognition of the similarities and differences and recognise the significance of these similarities and differences.	**Compare** archaea to bacteria.
Consider	Think deliberately or carefully about something, typically before making a decision; take something into account when making a judgment.	**Consider** why it is essential that foetal haemoglobin has a higher affinity for oxygen than adult haemoglobin.
Contrast	Display recognition of differences by deliberate juxtaposition of contrary elements; show how things are different or opposite; give an account of the differences between two or more items or situations, referring to both or all of them throughout.	**Contrast** an action spectrum and an absorption spectrum.
Deduce	Reach a conclusion that is necessarily true, provided a given set of assumptions is true; arrive at, reach or draw a logical conclusion from reasoning and the information given.	**Deduce** why the stomach contents are acidic.
Describe	Give an account (written or spoken) of a situation, event, pattern or process, or of the characteristics or features of something.	**Describe** how a protein differs from a polypeptide.

Cognitive verb	Definition	Sample question
Design	Produce a plan, simulation, model or similar; plan, form or conceive in the mind; in English, select, organise and use particular elements in the process of text construction for particular purposes; these elements may be linguistic (words), visual (images), audio (sounds), gestural (body language), spatial (arrangement on the page or screen) and multimodal (a combination of more than one).	**Design** a poster on the process of gel electrophoresis.
Determine	Establish, conclude or ascertain after consideration, observation, investigation or calculation; decide or come to a resolution.	**Determine** reasons why the ability to detect sugars is more sensitive than detection of other organic chemicals in many animals.
Discuss	Examine by argument; sift the considerations for and against; debate; talk or write about a topic, including a range of arguments, factors or hypotheses; consider, taking into account different issues and ideas, points for and/or against, and supporting opinions or conclusions with evidence.	**Discuss** how this mechanism may help quadrupeds to travel large distances at speed.
Evaluate	Make an appraisal by weighing up or assessing strengths, implications and limitations; make judgments about ideas, solutions or methods in relation to selected criteria; examine and determine the merit, value or significance of something, based on criteria.	**Evaluate** these two species and discuss which you would expect to be more successful in an arid region.
Explain	Make an idea or situation plain or clear by describing it in more detail or revealing relevant facts; give an account; provide additional information.	**Explain** the functions of DNA and RNA.
Identify	Distinguish; locate, recognise and name; establish or indicate who or what someone or something is; provide an answer from a number of possibilities; recognise and state a distinguishing factor or feature.	**Identify** the three components of a nucleotide.
Interpret	Use knowledge and understanding to recognise trends and draw conclusions from given information; make clear or explicit; elucidate or understand in a particular way; identify or draw meaning from, or give meaning to, information presented in various forms, such as words, symbols, pictures or graphs.	**Interpret** the graph to comment on the biological significance of the relationship between the action spectrum and the absorption spectrum.
Investigate	Carry out an examination or formal inquiry in order to establish or obtain facts and reach new conclusions; search, inquire into, interpret and draw conclusions about data and information.	**Investigate** the use of genetically modified crops to grow in the arid regions of Africa.
Justify	Give reasons or evidence to support an answer, response or conclusion; show how an argument, statement or conclusion is right or reasonable.	**Justify** why the current cell theory is more detailed than that proposed by Schleiden and Schwann.
Predict	Give an expected result of an upcoming action or event; infer what may happen based on available information.	**Predict** whether the 5% glucose solution will be hypertonic, hypotonic or approximately isotonic.
Propose	Put forward (e.g. a point of view, idea, argument, inference) for consideration or action.	Digestion of chunks of food is either within a food vacuole or extracellular. **Propose** possible reasons for this phenomenon.
Select	Choose in preference to another or others; pick out.	**Select** an appropriate method for sampling a population of ants in leaf litter.
Sketch	Execute a drawing or painting in simple form, giving essential features but not necessarily with detail or accuracy; in mathematics, represent by means of a diagram or graph; the sketch should give a general idea of the required shape or relationship and should include features.	**Sketch** a timeline of the five mass extinctions on earth.

1.2 Data test

There will be two to four datasets to consider and evaluate in this 1 hour exam. These data may be **qualitative**, such as a statement about whether a population of emus is present or not in a select location, or they may be **quantitative**, such as the final population of emus in a select location of Western Australia. The types of questions will include short-response items (from single-word or sentence responses, up to short-paragraph responses (fewer than 50 words). There will also be calculation-type questions, as well as questions requiring interpretation of datasets. Ten minutes of reading time at the beginning has been allowed for this task, followed by 60 minutes of writing time.

A graphics calculator is allowed. A list of key formulas is also permitted, so students should concentrate on how to use the formulas, rather than on memorising this material.

Here are some key tips:

- Read the questions carefully. Be particularly wary of reading a question and assuming it is identical to something that has been seen before, only to realise the error when it is too late to fix.
- Do not state a conclusion without also outlining the evidence used to reach that conclusion. Watch out for giving evidence that is merely the conclusion stated in a different way, e.g. 'The organism was a phototroph because it used sunlight for energy.'
- Mention any limits on the degree of certainty with which conclusions can be drawn, if these exist. If certain assumptions need to be made to reach a conclusion, then state these. For example, 'It was assumed that the temperature was constant throughout the experiment.'

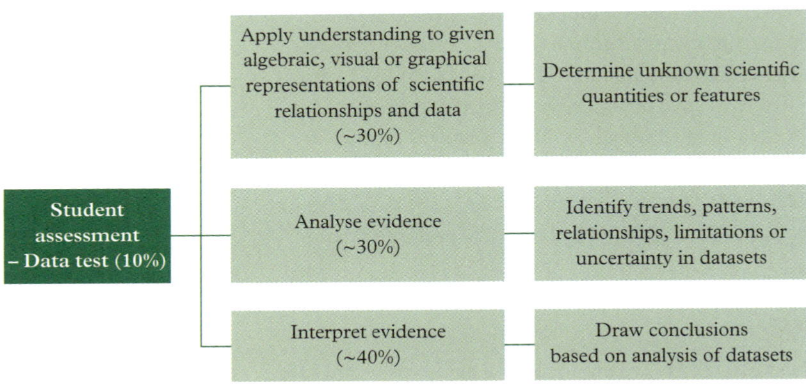

FIGURE 1 A graphical outline of the components of the Data test

DATA DRILL 1

Calibrating laboratory equipment

1 Laboratory incubators are used to grow microorganisms, such as fungi and bacteria. A calibration of an incubator was carried out using temperature probes.

Set temperature	Actual temperature
10°	11.5°
25°	28.75°
37°	42.55°

Calculate what percentage error the incubator is out of range by.

2 Laboratories use a range of different weighing balances for different purposes, including some that measure to 0.0 g down to 0.00 g, or even 0.000 g for very small quantities.

Select either 0.0 g or 0.00 g for the following samples.

Sample	Balance (0.0 g, 0.00 g)
Small amounts of pharmaceutical compounds	
Solid materials of a kilogram or more	
A small marsupial	
Wind-blown seeds	

3 An autoclave is a large steam oven, and is used to sterilise biological laboratory waste so that it can be disposed of safely. For an autoclave to successfully sterilise the contents, it needs to produce steam and maintain a temperature of at least 121°C and a pressure of at least 100 kPa for at least 15 minutes. This is to ensure that no life survives and that the equipment is completely sterile.

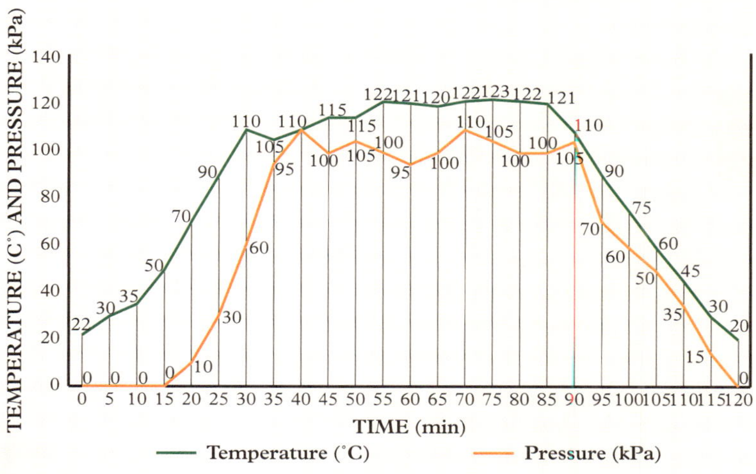

FIGURE 2 Temperature graph of an autoclave's cycle

a **Determine** if the autoclave run in Figure 2 was successful in sterilising the waste.

b **Consider** why larger loads may need a longer cycle in an autoclave.

1.3 Student experiment

This assessment is quite different from the other assessment items, as it requires the collection, analysis and synthesis of primary data. In other words, experiments must be planned and carried out to generate the data that will then be used/put together to answer a question or to confirm (or reject) a hypothesis related to biodiversity or ecosystem dynamics. This will take place over a period of 10 hours of class time, so it will be important to prepare a timeline for the project, remembering to allow time for the things that won't go according to plan, or will take longer than expected. The planning of the experiment will require research and thinking about how to conduct the experiment, and flexibility in adapting the experiment as challenges are identified. Students can sometimes be frustrated that experiments do not work properly the first time or give unclear results. It is important to learn how to trouble-shoot, to think clearly about what might be going wrong, and to adjust the experiment accordingly. This may require going back and re-doing experiments. Spending adequate time in the research and planning phase may enable some mis-steps to be avoided.

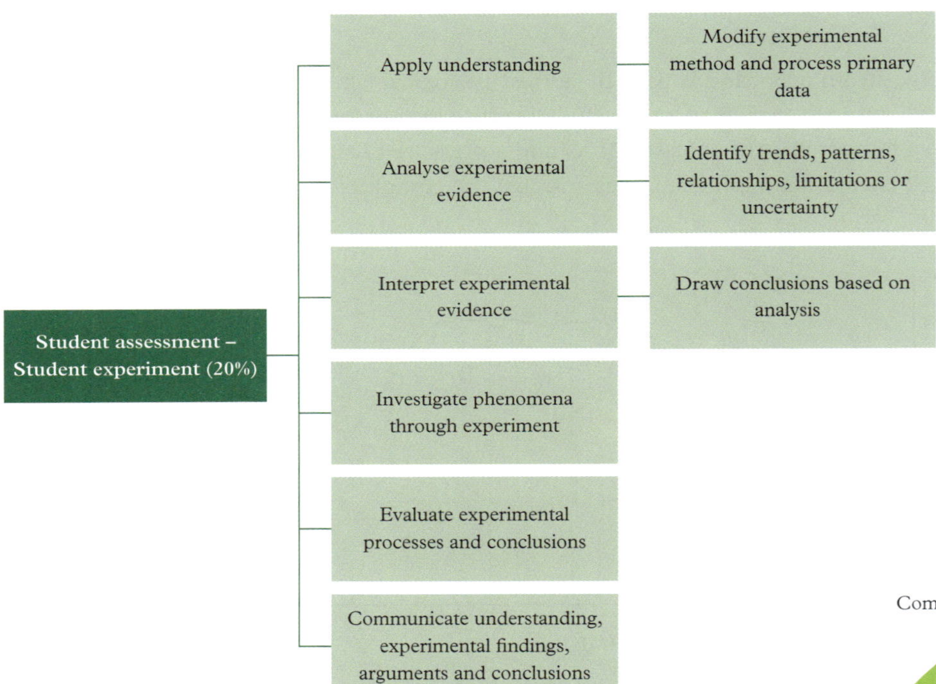

FIGURE 3 A graphical summary of the Student experiment

The experimental data, results, findings and conclusion then need to be communicated. This may be in a written format, such as a scientific report of between 1500 and 2000 words, or in a different format, such as a scientific poster or an oral presentation of 9–11 minutes. Not all aspects of the report are weighted equally. Tips on how to write a high-quality scientific report can be found in the *Biology for Queensland An Australian Perspective Units 3 & 4* Student Book.

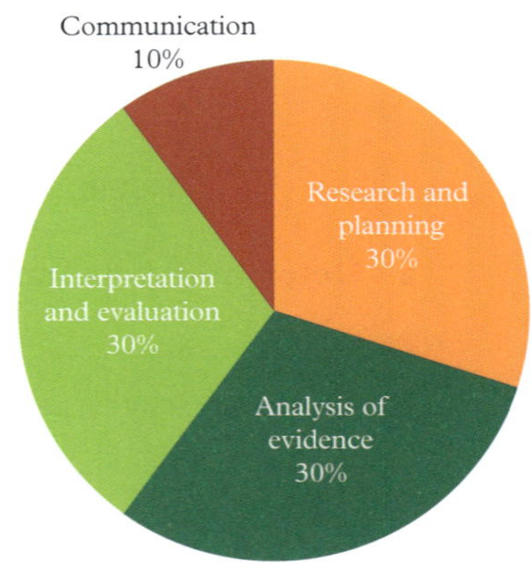

FIGURE 4 The mark breakdown of the elements in the Student experiment

EXPERIMENT EXPLORER 1

Writing a sound experiment

A class of students travelled to a local reserve to conduct quadrat measurements on the grass area near the foreshore.

Student report

Name: ______________________________

Date: 12 September

Using the quadrat method to monitor Beach Park reserve

Aim

We travelled to Beach Park reserve to take quadrats of the weeds growing near the shore.

Metarials

A quadrat for each group

We threw down the quadrat and recorded how many weeds and other stuff was in the quadrat.

Results

The 1st quadrat had 5 weeds of significance in them. The 2nd had 17, probably becouse it was near a tap. The 3rd had 8 weeds. I didn't get data for the 4th, partner was supposed to send me results afterwards and didn't. 5th quadrat had only 1 weed.

Conclusion

There are more weeds near water sources.

1 **Construct** a set of guidelines for this student to help them improve their experimental reports.

1.4 Research investigation

In the Research investigation task, students are required to evaluate a **claim**, by 'researching, analysing and interpreting **secondary evidence** from scientific texts' to justify a conclusion about the claim.

In the Student experiment students used primary evidence, i.e. data from experiments that they carried out. 'Secondary evidence' here means reports of findings and conclusions by other people, such as scientific articles published in journals. Reviews of original research can also be used as they can provide an interpretation or summary of the current state of knowledge in a particular area. The authors of secondary evidence will have made judgments about what the most important research findings are.

The evidence used for this task is required to come from scientifically credible sources. These may be scientific journals, books written by experts in the area, reports or websites of government bodies such as the CSIRO (Commonwealth Scientific and Industrial Research Organisation), or technical information provided by biological supplier companies or instrument makers.

There are some key elements essential to starting this task well:

- **Selecting a claim to be evaluated.** This may require some background general research first. Your teacher will provide guidance when you are selecting your claim.
- **Coming up with a research strategy by identifying the relevant scientific concepts that connect with the claim.** A lot of time could be lost by not having a plan for the research.
- **Constructing a research question.** The research question needs to be succinct and able to provide timely results.

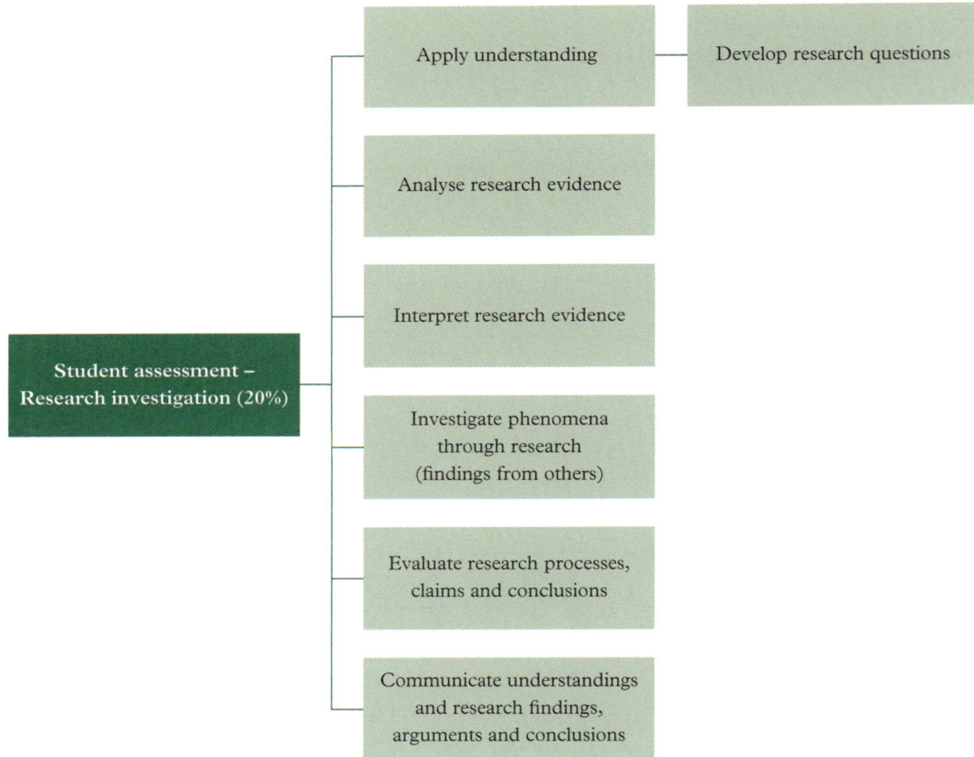

FIGURE 5 Key aspects of the Research investigation assessment

RESEARCH REVIEW 1

Becoming a good researcher

Many scientific researchers have considered the qualities a researcher needs to be successful. Below are a number of top tips from biogeochemist and researcher Dr Ellen Moon.

Keep detailed records (maybe including photos, written notes, audio notes) on everything you do. Don't fall into the trap of thinking you'll remember how many millilitres of reagent X you added, or what the room temperature was exactly. While this is especially important with lab work, it's also true of data analysis (why did you choose a particular statistical test or line of best fit?) and readings (where did you find that useful article?).

Be open to change. Research rarely goes the way we intend, and part way through your investigation it may make sense to shift your focus, to bring in a new technique, or even to try a completely different methodology. Your research plan isn't set in stone!

Embrace failure! Failure isn't the opposite of success – it's the other side of the same coin. We all make mistakes, and sometimes these can set us back during our research. But by learning from our mistakes, and designing strategies to overcome them, we can become better researchers.

1 **Reflect** on the kind of researcher you are by placing an 'X' on each line below.

Organised and tidy

FIGURE 6 Dr Ellen Moon

UNIT 3 Biodiversity and the interconnectedness of life

PRACTICALS IN THIS UNIT

	MANDATORY PRACTICAL, SUGGESTED PRACTICAL AND MANIPULATIVE SKILLS	**3.8A** Analysing vegetation patterns using a transect line
	MANDATORY PRACTICAL	**3.8B** Stratified sampling of vegetation patterns
	SUGGESTED PRACTICAL	**4.1A** A simplified food chain in leaf litter
	SUGGESTED PRACTICAL	**4.1B** Measuring biomass
	SUGGESTED PRACTICAL	**5.1** Plant distribution and abundance using quadrats
	SUGGESTED PRACTICAL	**5.4A** Competitive exclusion in *Paramecium*
	SUGGESTED PRACTICAL	**5.4B** Relationship between predator and prey
	SUGGESTED PRACTICAL	**5.5** Population study of yeast
	MANDATORY PRACTICAL	**6.4** Appraisal of an ecological surveying technique

WORD WIZARD

Draw a line to match each term with the correct definition.

ABIOTIC	Major classification group of the animal kingdom
DIVISION	Biomass of an organism at any particular moment
PHYLUM	Necessary and positive association between two organisms
POPULATION GROWTH	Increase in the size of a population in a particular habitat over time
PREDATION	The non-living physical factors that affect an organism's ability to survive
GENERALIST FEEDER	An organism that can utilise a range of nutrients; both herbivorous and carnivorous
STANDING CROP	Feeding of one organism (predator) on another (prey)
PIONEER SPECIES	Climax forest formed due to secondary succession
SECONDARY FOREST	Species of plants that colonise bare ground
PRODUCTIVITY	A heterotroph with a varied diet
MUTUALISM	Major classification group of the plants, fungi and plant-like protists
OMNIVORE	Amount of energy fixed in organic compounds; measured by increase of biomass per unit time
BIODIVERSITY	All the species which occupy a particular place at any particular time
COMMUNITY	The range of living organism and their environments

CHAPTER

2 Biodiversity

This chapter defines the term 'biodiversity', and recognises that biodiversity includes the diversity of species and ecosystems. The concepts of biological classification systems, such as the Linnaean biological classification, binomial naming system and dichotomous keys, are explored through real-world applications and scenarios. The role of nuclear and mitochondrial DNA analysis in the determination of a species and its evolutionary ancestry is explored through the use of cladistics. A study of the internal and external structures of organisms will be made in relation to their environment and ancestry. Finally, a comprehensive review of why multiple definitions of species are necessary is discussed.

CHAPTER CHECKLIST

Read this checklist before you complete this chapter's activities and then return to it to check your understanding before your assessments.

Once you have completed this chapter, you can use the 'I can …' statements to assess your understanding of the topics covered by ticking the appropriate box in the 'rating column'.

I can …	Confidently	Partially	Not really
… understand the different ecosystems			
… explain the Linnaean biological classification			
… define a species			
… understand the different ways of classifying an organism			
… explain cladistics			

DATA DRILL 2

Similarity of big cats

The genetic similarities of the big cats can be tested through DNA hybridisation. The following data were obtained during the DNA hybridisation of five big cats, using multiple genetic samples.

TABLE 1 Percentage difference between big cat species genomes via DNA hybridisation

	Snow leopard	Leopard	Jaguar	Lion	Tiger
Snow leopard	0.2	0.7	1.8	2.7	2.9
Leopard	0.7	0.2	2.1	2.8	2.9
Jaguar	1.8	2.1	0.2	1.3	1.2
Lion	2.7	2.8	1.3	0.2	0.5
Tiger	2.9	2.9	1.2	0.5	0.2

1 a **Determine** which of the big cat species are most closely related from the data in Table 1, and **explain** why. (**Hint**: The higher the percentage difference, the less related the two species are.)

FIGURE 1 A snow leopard is related to the other big cats, but how closely?

b Using the cladogram below, **identify** the two big cat species that are missing.

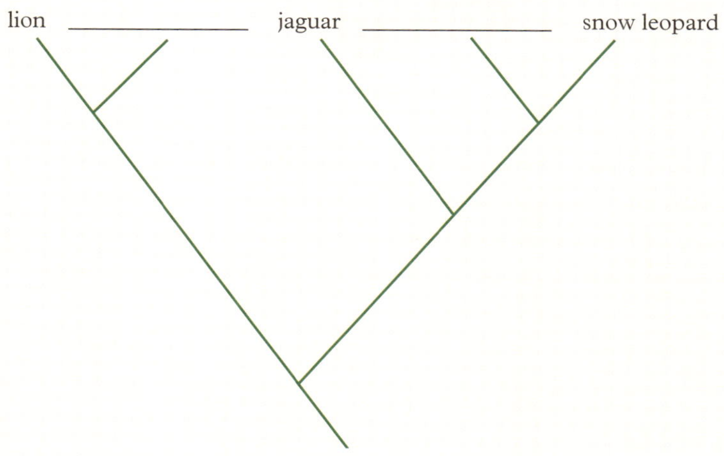

EXPERIMENT EXPLORER 2

Selecting the correct fieldwork equipment

When analysing an ecosystem and measuring abiotic factors, there are many instruments available for collecting data. Deciding which data are important and relevant to a study is vital for a successful experiment.

TABLE 2 Abiotic instruments and their uses

Instrument	Image	Description
pH meter		Used to measure the pH of solutions. Soil pH tests can also be conducted. Units: pH
Thermometer		Used to measure the temperature of air and liquids, the temperature probe can also be inserted into soft material, e.g. soil. Units: degrees Celsius (°C)
Dissolved oxygen meter		Used to measure the amount of dissolved oxygen in liquids. Units: ppt (parts per thousand)
Salinity meter		Used to measure the salt concentration of liquids. Units: electrical conductivity (EC) or ppm (parts per million)

1 An ecologist is studying a stretch of river in the Daintree Rainforest in North Queensland, and is taking a series of measurements to categorise the ecosystem for future studies.

a The ecologist decides to measure the relevant abiotic factors of the river water itself. **Decide** which instruments and measurements would be relevant from the list above.

____

____

____

b The ecologist continues upriver and finds a native orchid, previously thought to be extinct. The native bee that pollinates the orchid has been declared endangered. The ecologist marks the location of the orchid, so that it can be found again, and measures the abiotic factors surrounding it. **Determine** the abiotic factors the ecologist should measure.

RESEARCH REVIEW 2

Choose your audience

We change the way we write and speak depending on the audience we're communicating with. The way we speak on social media can be very different from how we would speak in a job interview, or chat at a family dinner.

Scientists must also consider the way they communicate to make sure they are targeting the correct audience. Communicating their findings to fellow scientists requires a different tone to that needed for communicating their findings to the public.

FIGURE 2 Speaking to a crowd

1 **Develop** a set of guidelines for a new scientist on how their findings can best be communicated to the general public.

Study tip

Binomial scientific names in which the genus or species name ends with i, ia or ii are usually named after their discoverer, rather than describing the organism itself. Banksia trees (*Banksia* spp.) don't necessarily grow on the banks of rivers, and Children's pythons (*Antaresia childreni*) are not named for their love of children!

EXAM EXCELLENCE 2

Multiple choice – circle the correct answer

1 Define biodiversity.

A a biological community of interacting organisms and their physical environment

B the range of living organisms and their ecosystems

C a grouping of organisms in terms of similarities in morphology, anatomy and biochemistry

D a method of grouping organisms that uses evolutionary lines of descent rather than structural similarities

2 Which of the following organisms are most closely related?

A *Cordyline rubra* (palm lily) and *Haliotis rubra* (blacklip abalone)

B *Crocodylus porosus* (saltwater crocodile) and *Alligator missisippiensis* (American alligator)

C *Equus zebra* (zebra) and *Equus ferus caballus* (horse)

D *Canis lupus dingo* (dingo) and *Canis lupus familiaris* (domestic dog)

3 Which of the following cladogram is **not** an example of a clade?

A

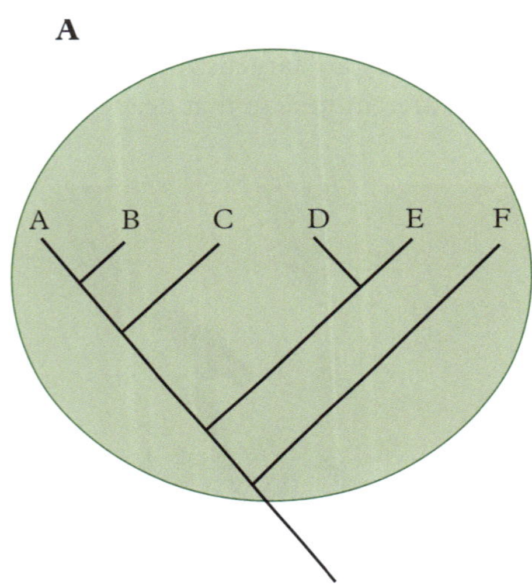

B

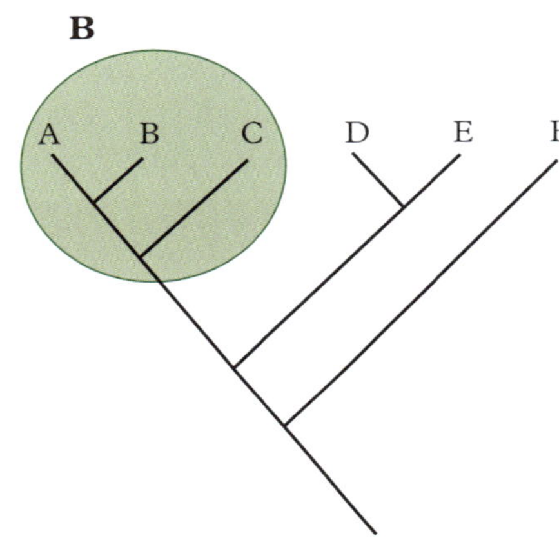

C

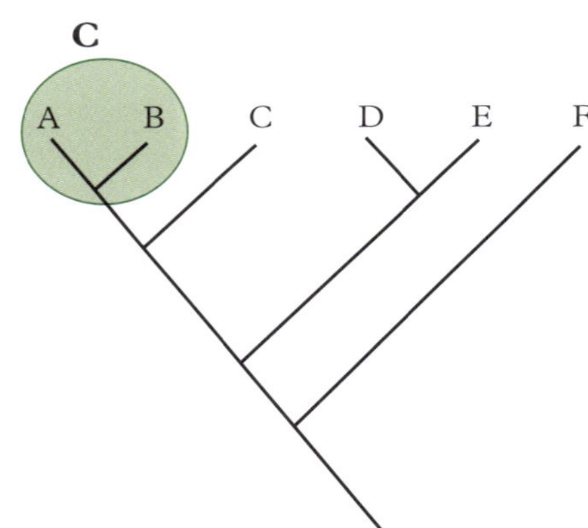

D

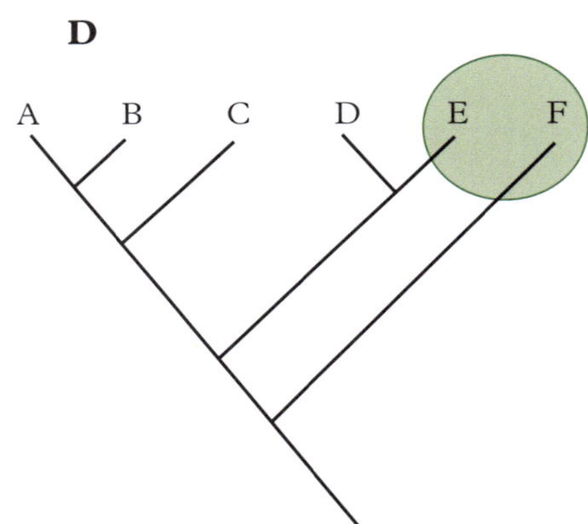

4 Which of the following statements about DNA hybridisation is true?

A If the chains of hybridised DNA separate at a high temperature, the species is most likely closely related.

B DNA molecules are bound by covalent bonds.

C If the chains of hybridised DNA separate at a low temperature, the species is most likely closely related.

D Partial hybridisation indicates that organisms are most likely unrelated.

5 Which of the following statements is **not** true when comparing analysis of mitochondrial DNA (mtDNA) with that of nuclear DNA to determine species relationships?

A Mitochondria are present in large numbers in each cell, so fewer cell samples are required to obtain large amounts of mtDNA.

B mtDNA does not exhibit recombination of its genetic material.

C mtDNA has a lower rate of mutation than nuclear DNA, making it easier to trace back the lineage of an organism on its maternal side.

D Direct genetic lines can be traced, since only maternal mtDNA is passed on to offspring.

Short answer

6 The Linnaean biological system of classification relies on a number of characteristics to identify living things.

TABLE 3 Classification of organisms

Domain	Archaea	Bacteria	Eukarya			
Kingdom	**Archaebacteria**	**Eubacteria**	**Protista**		**Plantae**	**Animalia**
Characteristics	Distinguished on the basis of rRNA and cell wall composition					
Cell type		Prokaryote	Eukaryote	Eukaryote	Eukaryote	Eukaryote
Chloroplasts	Absent		Present in some forms	Absent	Present	Absent
Mode of nutrition	Heterotrophs or chemosynthetic autotrophs	Heterotrophs that require oxygen or autotrophs (photosynthesis)	Photosynthesis or heterotrophic or combination of both	Heterotrophic by absorption		Heterotrophic by ingestion
Multi-cellularity	Absent	Absent	Present except in yeasts		Present	Present
Locomotion	Absent	Absent in most	Absent	Absent	Absent	
Nervous system	Absent	Absent		Absent	Absent	Present except in sponges

a **Identify** the gaps in Table 3 and provide the correct answer.

b **Justify** the division of Kingdom Plantae into Kingdom Plantae and Kingdom Fungi in 1959.

7 Before European settlement, Indigenous Australians and Torres Strait Islander peoples named the plants and animals around them according to beliefs, taboos and food usage. Today, scientists use a worldwide classification system for naming organisms.

a **Explain** the importance of naming plants and animals in pre-European Australia.

b **Discuss** why scientists today use a worldwide system for classification.

8 Mules, ligers and wholphins are examples of hybrid organisms.

a **Define** the characteristics of a hybrid organism.

b **Explain** whether a liger would have a species name.

9 Taxonomists use internal and external structures of organisms to classify them.

a **Contrast** homologous structures and analogous structures.

b **Determine** which of the following are homologous structures and which are analogous structures.

i a bird wing and a bat wing

ii a bird wing and an insect wing

iii a bird wing and a fish fin

10 A customs officer discovers an adult python loose at Brisbane International Airport and writes a report.

> **Incident**
>
> Snake found in baggage reclaim near carousel 6, international arrivals level 2. Type of python. Approx. 1.5 m brown mottled. Snake catcher retrieved it and took it to quarantine labs at 5:30 pm Tuesday.
>
> Signed

a From the report, **assess** which information is important in identifying the snake and its possible origin.

b **Use** the dichotomous key below to **determine** whether this species is native to Queensland or has possibly come from overseas.

TABLE 4 Identifying python species in Queensland

Key to python species in Queensland		
1 Black head and neck	*Aspidites melanocephalus*	Black-headed python
Head similar colour to body	Go to 2.	
2 Spotted	*Antaresia maculosa*	Spotted python
Other marking	Go to 3.	
3 Mottled	Go to 4.	
Striped	*Aspidites ramsayi*	Woma python
4 Tan and dark-brown mottling	Go to 5.	
White and black mottling	*Morelia spilota*	Diamond python
5 Adult length ≤ 1 metre	*Antaresia childreni*	Children's python
Adult length > 1 metre	*Unknown*	Unknown

c Imported reptiles are not permitted in Australia unless for zoological purposes under controlled conditions. **Discuss** the possible effects on local ecosystems that an introduced reptile (e.g. python) could have.

CHAPTER 3

Biological interactions

This chapter explores the interactions between organisms in their environment, whether it be between members of the same species (intraspecific), within a community of species (interspecific), or between organisms and their environment (biotic and abiotic factors). The roles of consumers, producers, decomposers and detritivores in an ecosystem are discussed.

Individuals within a population of a species may compete for resources, mates and space, but they can also benefit through sharing the workload of collecting food, caring for young, and defending from predators.

Interspecies relationships, such as a mutually beneficial 'mutualism' relationship or a one-sided 'parasitic' relationship, are discussed via the concept of symbiosis.

Abiotic factors can limit the distribution and abundance of a species in an ecosystem, and this can be represented through optimal range and tolerance range graphs. Abiotic factors such as climate, soil and geography are discussed in depth.

Key methods of sampling and monitoring ecosystems are explored throughout the chapter, including the tools for analysing data from these methods, allowing students to determine the characteristics of aquatic and terrestrial environments and the factors that influence the life that exists there.

CHAPTER CHECKLIST

Read this checklist before you complete this chapter's activities then return to it to check your understanding before your assessments.

Once you have completed this chapter, you can use the 'I can …' statements to assess your understanding of the topics covered by ticking the appropriate box in the 'rating column'.

I can …	Confidently	Partially	Not really
… define and classify different ecosystems			
… contrast between biotic and abiotic factors			
… identify features in aquatic ecosystems			
… identify features in terrestrial ecosystems			
… calculate biodiversity and measure features in different ecosystems			

DATA DRILL 3

Species diversity of Australian parrots

As part of a national bird count program, two communities of parrots in south-east Queensland were sampled at two sites 100 km apart using net cannon sampling. The parrots were marked and released. The results are below.

TABLE 1 Results of national bird count program in south-east Queensland

Community A (Warrego River)		Community B (Lake Bindegolly)	
Species	**Number of individuals**	**Species**	**Number of individuals**
Melopsittacus undulatus (budgerigar)	152	*Melopsittacus undulatus* (budgerigar)	29
Nymphicus hollandicus (cockatiel)	12	*Nymphicus hollandicus* (cockatiel)	10
Lophochroa leadbeateri (Major Mitchell's cockatoo)	2	*Lophochroa leadbeateri* (Major Mitchell's cockatoo)	0
Aprosmictus erythropterus (red-winged parrot)	27	*Aprosmictus erythropterus* (red-winged parrot)	2

Simpson's Index (D) is the probability that two randomly selected individuals will be the same species.

$$D = \frac{\Sigma n(n-1)}{N(N-1)}$$

where n = total number of individuals of a particular species, N = total number of organisms of all species and $\Sigma\ n(n-1)$ is the sum of all species calculations of $n(n-1)$.

For example, if there are 3 birds, 2 mammals and 4 fish, the Simpson's Index calculation would be:

$$3(3-1) + 2(2-1) + 4(4-1)/9(9-1) = 0.28$$

This means there is a 28% chance that two randomly selected individuals will be the same species. Simpson's Diversity Index (SDI) is the probability that two randomly selected individuals will *not* be different species.

$$SDI = 1 - D$$

Continuing the previous example:

$$SDI = 1 - 0.28$$
$$SDI = 0.72$$

This means there is a 72% chance two randomly selected individuals will be different species.

1 **Use** Simpson's Diversity Index to **compare** the diversity of the two parrot communities.

Six months after the initial sampling, another sample was taken at the same location (the capture–recapture method) with the following results.

TABLE 2 Results of national bird count program in south-east Queensland 6 months later

Community A (Warrego River)			Community B (Lake Bindegolly)		
Species	Number of individuals total	Number of individuals marked	Species	Number of individuals total	Number of individuals marked
Melopsittacus undulatus (budgerigar)	128	12	*Melopsittacus undulatus* (budgerigar)	32	3
Nymphicus hollandicus (cockatiel)	18	1	*Nymphicus hollandicus* (cockatiel)	8	2
Lophochroa leadbeateri (Major Mitchell's cockatoo)	5	1	*Lophochroa leadbeateri* (Major Mitchell's cockatoo)	1	0
Aprosmictus erythropterus (red-winged parrot)	38	8	*Aprosmictus erythropterus* (red-winged parrot)	0	0

The Lincoln Index (N) is a way of estimating the size of a population using results from the capture, mark and recapture method of sampling.

$$N = \frac{M \times n}{m}$$

where M = number originally marked, n = total number captured in second sample, and m = number of marked individuals in second sample.

For example, when sampling a species of marsupials in traps, the first sampling captures five marsupials, which are all marked. They are then released and after a time the population is sampled again. Six marsupials are caught, with only one being already marked.

$$N = \frac{5 \times 6}{1}$$

Size of population (N) = 30

2 **Estimate** the size of the populations of budgerigar at both sites using the Lincoln Index calculation (rounded to the nearest 10).

EXPERIMENT EXPLORER 3

Behavioural adaptations of slaters

When exhibiting behavioural adaptations, animals possess the ability to make choices: whether to pursue prey or conserve their energy, whether to move into shade during the heat of the day or not, and whether to remain hidden when a predator is around or attempt to flee.

An experiment was conducted using slaters (*Armadillidium vulgare*) to determine their preference for two abiotic factors: light and moisture. Forty slaters were added to a choice chamber (shown at right), and their position was noted every minute for 15 minutes. The results are as follows.

FIGURE 1 A choice chamber for slaters

TABLE 3 Results of slater experiment

Time (min)	No. of slaters in 'light/dry'	No. of slaters in 'light/moist'	No. of slaters in 'dark/dry'	No. of slaters in 'dark/moist'
1	3	3	16	18
2	3	4	16	17
3	2	2	17	19
4	1	2	19	18
5	0	2	18	20
6	2	2	16	20
7	2	3	18	17
8	3	2	19	16
9	0	4	18	18
10	2	3	18	17
11	0	4	17	19
12	1	3	17	19
13	3	3	18	16
14	2	2	17	19
15	2	3	16	19

The scientist conducting the experiment concluded that, since most of the slaters were found in the dark section of the choice chamber most of the time, and there were approximately equal numbers in the 'dark and dry' and 'dark and moist' sections, the slaters preferred darkness but did not have a preference for moisture level.

FIGURE 2 A slater

1 **Plot** a graph of the data found on the previous page, remembering to give the graph a title and label the axes, and to include units. There should be four distinct lines on one graph.

RESEARCH REVIEW 3

Rules for making a good poster

A biology teacher is planning marking criteria for a good poster.

1 **Research** what makes a good poster and **identify** five main features that you should include when making a poster.

EXAM EXCELLENCE 3

Multiple choice – circle the correct answer

1 The channel-billed cuckoo is a species of bird that lays its eggs in the nests of other birds. Those birds raise the cuckoo chick while neglecting their own chicks, which eventually die, or are pushed out of the nest by the much larger cuckoo chick. Determine the type of relationship between the cuckoo and the adoptive parent birds.

A commensalism

B parasitism

C predation

D competition

2 Jardine River National Park, on Cape York Peninsula, receives 1417 mm of rain each year, with an evapotranspiration rate of 2033 mm. The potential evapotranspiration ratio is found by dividing the annual precipitation by the evapotranspiration rate. Determine what type of ecosystem Jardine River National Park is according to the Holdridge life zone system.

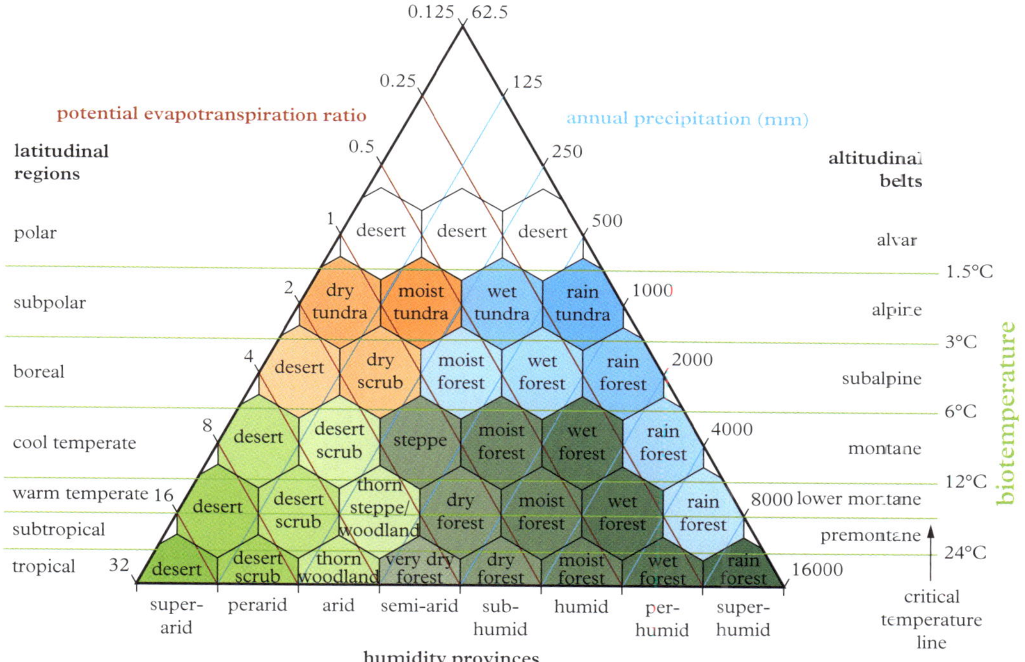

FIGURE 3 Holdridge life zone system

A rainforest

B desert scrub

C moist tundra

D moist forest

3 Explain the main difference between biomes and ecoregions.

A Biomes are mostly based on the community of organisms, while ecoregions are mostly based on geology, soil and climate types.

B Ecoregions are much larger than biomes, encompassing whole continents.

C A biome refers to the vegetation zone of an ecoregion.

D There is no difference between biomes and ecoregions, and the terms are used interchangeably.

4 The calculation for species diversity is:
  A EUNIS Index
  B Berlese-Tullgren Index
  C Lincoln Index
  D Simpson's Diversity Index

5 An example of mimicry is:
  A a stick insect appearing like a part of a plant
  B the stingless hoverfly that looks like a honeybee
  C the chameleon that can change colour to blend with the background
  D peppered moths in unpolluted environments being light in colour

Short answer

6 **Compare** tolerance range and optimum range.

7 **Contrast** freshwater and marine ecosystems by completing the table below.

	Freshwater	Marine
Movement of water between environment and organisms due to dissolved salts		
Depth		
Water pressure		
Water temperature variability		
Variety of organisms		

8 While travelling inland from a coastal town, an ecologist noted the characteristics of the surrounding vegetation. Near the coast, there were towering eucalyptus trees with an understorey of ferns and creepers (first zone). As the ecologist travelled further inland, there were fewer ferns and no creepers present (second zone). The ecologist reached the destination, where there were no trees present, and the main plants were grasses and semi-succulent, low-growing bushes (third zone).

a **Describe** the journey in terms of Australian vegetation zones.

b The ecologist noted that there was no intermediate transition between the second and third zones, only a fence line. **Infer** which zone/s may have been present between the second and third zones in the past.

9 **a** **Identify** two sampling methods used to analyse the invertebrate population of a woodland.

b **Determine** which method would be more appropriate for using in a desert environment.

10 In the space below, **sketch** a flowchart to illustrate how coral bleaching occurs.

CHAPTER 4

Functioning ecosystems

This chapter begins with a discussion of the transformation of solar energy into biomass and its transfer through the biotic components of an ecosystem. The conversion of solar energy into chemical energy through photosynthesis is the role of the producers, the plants, in ecosystems. Food webs are used to represent the transfer of that energy from the producers to the higher order consumers. They also show the role of the decomposers and detritivores.

Ecological pyramids are used to represent the number of organisms and the amount of biomass or energy at each trophic level. They are useful for making predictions about the health and future of an ecosystem.

Biogeochemical cycles describe the movement of elements through the biosphere, as well as the multiple transformations and transfers that they undergo. Elements are constantly exchanged between the environment and organisms. When in balance – that is, when the element is returned to the environment as rapidly as it is removed by living organisms – it is said to be a perfect cycle. This chapter explores water, oxygen, carbon and nitrogen cycles in depth.

Finally, the roles of keystone species, umbrella species and flagship species – and of conservation groups who aim to protect them – are highlighted in successful examples of humanity's pursuit to preserve functioning ecosystems.

CHAPTER CHECKLIST

Read this checklist before you complete this chapter's activities and then return to it to check your understanding before your assessments.

Once you have completed this chapter, you can use the 'I can …' statements to assess your understanding of the topics covered by ticking the appropriate box in the 'rating column'.

I can …	Confidently	Partially	Not really
… understand the different sources of energy in ecosystems			
… construct ecological pyramids			
… explain different biogeochemical cycles			
… define a keystone species			

DATA DRILL 4

Constructing ecological pyramids

The Daintree rainforest in far north Queensland is a biodiverse tropical ecosystem. Many species of birds, reptiles, mammals and invertebrates are found nowhere else in the world.

A study was undertaken in a small section of the Daintree rainforest: within a 1 km^2 area, the following organisms were counted.

Organism	Number	Average weight of each individual	Biomass
Flowering plants/trees	120	1000 kg	
Butterflies/moths	9000	5 g	
Insectivorous bats	400	25 g	
Snakes	5	1 kg	
Owls	1	1.5 kg	

1 a **Construct** a pyramid of organism numbers in the space below.

b **Calculate** the biomass of the organisms in this food chain and add your results to the table above. (**Hint**: Convert all units to the same type of unit when calculating biomass.)

c **Construct** a pyramid of the biomass of the organisms.

EXPERIMENT EXPLORER 4

Troubleshooting an experiment

Detecting errors in an experiment are important when assessing the validity of the method, data, and subsequent conclusion. The scientific method has many in-built checks to make sure an experiment is valid, and these are continually assessed.

1 **Discuss** why each of the following guidelines for an experiment is necessary.

Guidelines	Why this is necessary
Use SI units only.	
A hypothesis cannot change once the data are collected.	
Where possible, take multiple samples or run multiple tests on the same sample.	
Experiments should be repeatable under similar conditions.	
Results should be presented on a table or graph.	
Positive and negative controls should be used where possible in experiments.	
Only change one variable at a time.	

RESEARCH REVIEW 4

Reading abstracts

An abstract is a brief summary at the start of a scientific report that explains the aim, method and results of an investigation. This is valuable for other researchers to quickly determine whether reading the entire report would be useful for their current studies.

Consider the following abstract:

Reduced pesticide use increases the abundance of invertebrate predators in a monoculture cropping system

Author: Dr A, Dr B and Dr C

Publication: *Nature Science* January 2020

Abstract: The extensive use of pesticides has vastly decreased the numbers of invertebrates present in monoculture crops. However, stronger and stronger pesticides are required because the pest species become resistant to the pesticides. Corn, cotton and soybean crops are regularly afflicted with aphid infestations (corn aphids on corn, cotton aphids on cotton and so on). Our study followed 12 sites that reduced or halted the use of pesticides from 2015 to 2019 (six corn crops, two cotton crops and four soybean crops). Initially, there was an increase in the abundance of the various pest aphid species. This was followed by a marked increase in the number of arthropod predators, mostly ladybirds, spiders and lacewings. The numbers of aphids decreased dramatically and is now at manageable levels, with little damage and little loss of yield.

1 **Summarise** the main points in the abstract.

- ______
- ______
- ______
- ______

2 Assume a 10% biomass transfer between trophic levels. **Construct** a biomass pyramid for the cotton crop, cotton aphids and ladybirds, with the cotton aphids' mass at 150 kg.

EXAM EXCELLENCE 4

Multiple choice – circle the correct answer

1 Identify the type of energy in ecosystem food webs sourced from photosynthesis in plants.

A solar energy
B chemical energy
C heat energy
D nuclear energy

2 In a food chain and food web, arrows are used to represent relationships between organisms. Which of the following is true?

A Arrows are used to show which organism consumes which, e.g. frog → fly.
B Arrows are used to show the movement of energy through a food web, e.g. fly → frog.
C Arrows are used to show which organisms are decomposers.
D All arrows originate at the decomposers.

3 Which of the following is true for the pyramid of numbers to the right?

A The primary producer is very large.
B There are no tertiary consumers in this ecosystem.
C The primary producer is most likely grasses.
D This is most likely a desert ecosystem

FIGURE 1 Pyramid of numbers

4 Which of the following is **not** a role of bacteria in the nitrogen cycle?

A converting free nitrogen (N_2) into nitrates (NO_3)
B removing oxygen (O_2) from nitrates (NO_3)
C converting ammonia (NH_3) into nitrites (NO_2)
D converting free nitrogen (N_2) into ammonia (NH_3)

5 Which of the following classes of organisms will usually have the greatest biomass in a community?

A third order consumer
B second order consumer
C herbivores
D producers

Short answer

6 In the food chain below, the population of native mice declined rapidly due to a nearby baiting program on agricultural land.

FIGURE 2 A simple food chain

a **Determine** what effect a decline in the native mouse population would have on the grasses.

____

____

b **Determine** what effect a decline in the native mouse population would have on the snake population.

____

____

7 On a coral reef, there are 1 000 000 free-swimming multicellular algae. They are autotrophs and gain their energy from the sun via photosynthesis. For every 10 000 units of energy they gain, 2500 are used for growth and repair, and 7500 are lost as heat. The total weight of the algae in this area is 500 kg.

Approximately 50 000 zooplankton graze on the algae. They weigh 0.5 g each. For every 500 units of energy they consume, only 100 are used for growth and repair, and the rest is lost as heat. A school of 100 fish feed on the zooplankton. They consume 10 units of energy, 5 of which are lost as heat. The fish weigh 50 g each. An octopus that lives in the coral reef weighs 1 kg. It feeds on the fish in the area. Of the 2 units of energy it consumes, 1 is lost as heat and the other is used on growing.

In the space below, **sketch** the:

a pyramid by numbers	b biomass pyramid	c energy pyramid

8 Macronutrients cycling through ecosystems have two phases: a reservoir pool and a cycling pool. **Organise** the information below by drawing lines to connect each nutrient with the correct reservoir and cycling pool.

Reservoir pool	Nutrients	Cycling pool
Metallic compounds	Water	Photosynthesis – respiration
Deep-sea sediments	Oxygen	Nitrogen fixation – denitrification
Phosphate rock; deep-sea sediments	Carbon	Erosion – uptake – phosphatising
Artesian; glaciers; polar ice caps	Nitrogen	Respiration – photosynthesis
Fossils; peat; coal; oil and gas; trees	Phosphorus	Transpiration – evaporation – precipitation – uptake

9 Review the diagram of the carbon cycle below. **Determine** the missing items at points A–D:

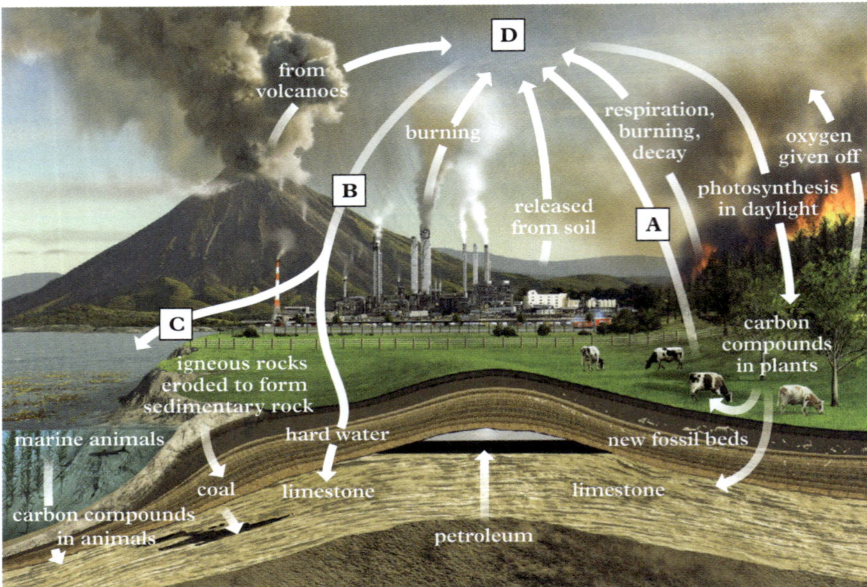

FIGURE 3 The carbon cycle

A ____________________

B ____________________

C ____________________

D ____________________

10 The southern cassowary, flying fox and northern quoll are considered keystone species in their ecosystems.

a **Define** the term 'keystone species'.

b In the space below, **explain** what makes each of these species a keystone species.

Southern cassowary	Flying fox

CHAPTER 5

Populations

This chapter examines the distribution and abundance of a species in a particular region, giving an overall view of the population density for that species. Both distribution and abundance are affected by biotic and abiotic factors in the ecosystem. Different patterns of distribution are discussed, and a method for calculating population density is given.

Population size can vary significantly over time. A population growth rate takes into consideration not only the birth rate of the population, but the death rate, immigration rate and emigration rate as well. Population growth curves can be analysed; when the limiting factors of a population are known, predictions of population growth can be made. These limiting factors can include those independent of the growth rate (such as environmental disasters and pollution) and those affected by the population density (such as predation and competition).

Two reproductive strategies evolved by many species are discussed: those of the *r*-strategists and the *K*-strategists. *r*-strategists produce large numbers of offspring but have little parental involvement in raising them; many of these offspring become victims of predation before reaching adulthood. In contrast, *K*-strategists are long-lived, with few offspring but extensive parental involvement in raising them to adulthood.

Finally, a comprehensive view of how populations are maintained through ecological homeostasis is explored.

CHAPTER CHECKLIST

Read this checklist before you complete this chapter's activities then return to it to check your understanding before your assessments.

Once you have completed this chapter, you can use the 'I can …' statements to assess your understanding of the topics covered by ticking the appropriate box in the 'rating column'.

I can …	Confidently	Partially	Not really
… understand the difference between distribution and abundance			
… explain population growth and its strategies			
… understand density-dependent factors			
… understand carrying capacity			

DATA DRILL 5

Human population

The latest human population on Earth has been estimated at 7.7 billion by the United Nations in December 2018. The years for each billion milestone reached are found below.

TABLE 1 Billion milestones of the human population

Year	1804	1930	1960	1974	1987	1999	2011
Population milestone	1 billion	2 billion	3 billion	4 billion	5 billion	6 billion	7 billion

1 a Construct the population growth curve in the space below.

b Consider what effect the following events could have on the population growth rate of an area.

i mass vaccination programs ______________________________

____

ii war ______________________________

____

iii famine and drought ______________________________

____

iv contraception ______________________________

____

Study tip

Although creating a graph will help you interpret data for all of your internal assessments, it is not assessed in the Data test.

EXPERIMENT EXPLORER 5

Under laboratory conditions

When biological experiments are conducted in a laboratory, they are done so under standard laboratory conditions, which are a standard set of abiotic conditions used in a laboratory setting. These are a temperature of 25°C and an air pressure of 100 kPa.

1 List the benefits of conducting biological experiments under laboratory conditions, and give an example of one experiment where this would be suitable.

2 A new mesophilic bacterium species is found in the human digestive tract, and a microbiologist wants to grow the bacteria on agar plates for further study. The bacteria are grown at 37°C on a nutrient agar plate.
Compare the two environments: that of the digestive tract and that of the agar plate.

FIGURE 1 A biological agar plate containing a new mesophilic bacterium

RESEARCH REVIEW 5

Identifying trends in data

Identifying trends in scientific data is an important aspect of research. Identifying trends can allow you to make predictions about values that are outside the scope of the experiment. For example, if data show a population increasing at a particular rate, predictions can be made about where the population could be in the near future. An identified trend in scientific data may not come from a single dataset. It could come from multiple datasets measuring multiple factors.

When a saltwater crocodile (*Crocodylus porosus*) lays a clutch of eggs, the temperature of the nest determines the sex of the offspring. Cooler nests (below 31°C) will produce more female offspring. Above 31°C, the offspring are more likely to be all males.

Several saltwater crocodiles occupy territory in a stretch of a North Queensland river. The sexes of the offspring in multiple nest sites have been recorded over a 10-year period. The area has been under severe drought since 2013.

1 **a** **Construct** a graph from the following data to determine whether there is a trend in the data.

TABLE 2 Numbers of female and male offspring in nest sites of saltwater crocodiles in a North Queensland river

Offspring	2010	2011	2012	2013	2014	2015	2016	2017	2018	2019
Female	10	8	8	7	7	5	5	4	5	3
Male	9	8	9	8	10	8	9	7	7	8
Total	19	16	17	15	17	13	14	11	12	11

b The level of water in the river has dropped during the study, as seen in the graph below.

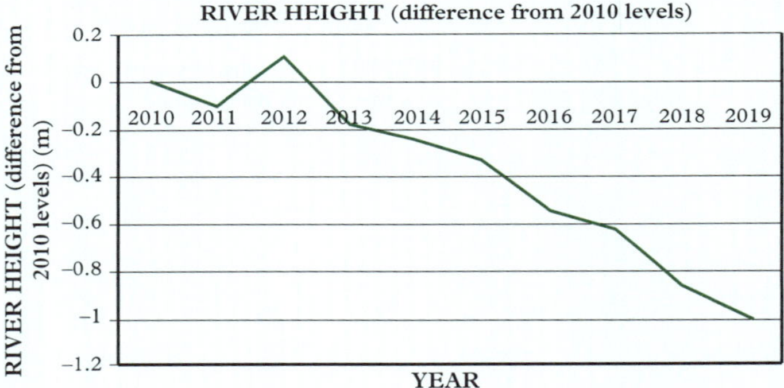

FIGURE 2 Changes in water level of a river in North Queensland

FIGURE 3 A crocodile hatchling

Summarise the possible causes of the trends seen in both the sex of crocodile hatchlings and the number of offspring hatched.

____

____

____

____

____

EXAM EXCELLENCE 5

Multiple choice – circle the correct answer

1 A species shows the following distribution pattern. What type of distribution pattern is shown in Figure 4?

A random

B clumped

C even

D solitary

FIGURE 4 Distribution pattern of a species

2 Which of the following is **not** a density-independent factor?

A water

B competition

C nutrients

D sunlight

3 What are light, temperature, water, nutrients, environmental disasters, food supply, availability of mates and competition all examples of?

A density-dependent factors

B density-independent factors

C limiting factors

D population growth

4 Butterflies and moths occupy the same niche in an ecosystem. They are both nectar feeders and prefer the same conditions. Butterflies feed during the day, and moths feed during the night. In a particular ecosystem, both populations have a healthy number of organisms. Determine which population concept is being demonstrated here.

A competitive exclusion principle

B resource partitioning

C biotic potential

D carrying capacity

5 Determine how environmental resistance affects carrying capacity.

A Environmental resistance increases the carrying capacity for a population.

B Environmental resistance limits the carrying capacity for a population.

C Environmental resistance and carrying capacity are not linked.

D Environmental resistance and carrying capacity are the same and the terms are used interchangeably.

Short answer

6 Penguins of the Antarctic Peninsula are one of the few types of organisms to exhibit even spacing distribution of their nesting sites.

a **Explain** why even spacing of nest sites would be beneficial for penguin colonies living in Antarctica.

FIGURE 5 Distribution of nesting perguins on the Antarctic Peninsula

b Other species that live in coastal regions, such as seals and cormorants, also exhibit even spacing distribution within their colonies. Deduce which feature of the landscape would promote even spacing.

7 **Compare** the positive and negative effects of a flooding event on an ecosystem.

8 **a** **Calculate** the population growth rate, per day, for an invertebrate species when there are 220 births, 0 immigrants, 126 deaths and 7 emigrants within one day.

The population growth rate was calculated again 6 months later and found to be 65/day.

b **Determine** which portion (A, B, C or D) of the growth rate graph this population is most likely in.

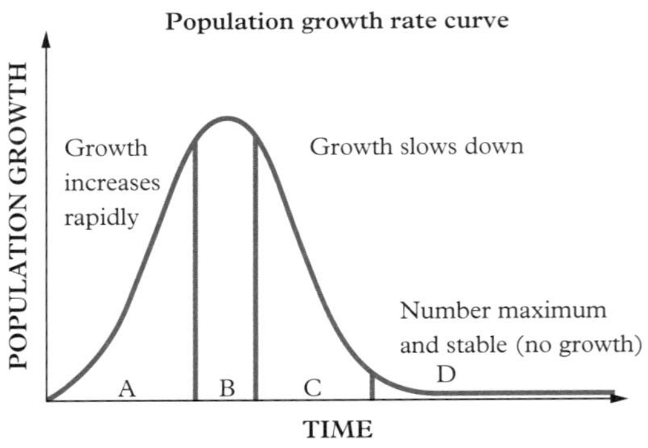

FIGURE 6 Population growth rate curve

9 a Discuss why the *r*- and *K*-strategists theory could be considered a spectrum rather than two discrete categories of organisms.

b Give an example of an organism not listed that exhibits characteristics of both *r*-strategists and *K*-strategists. **Explain** your reasoning in depth with an example.

10 Consider Figure 7 below.

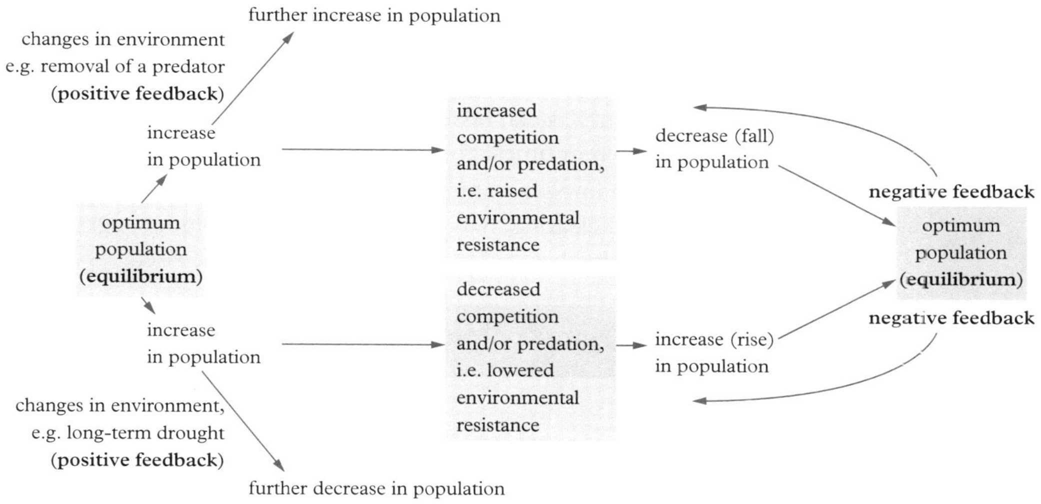

FIGURE 7 Homeostatic control of population growth

a Describe two changes in environment (other than removal of a predator) that would lead to an increase in a population.

b Describe two changes in environment (other than long-term drought) that would lead to a decrease in a population.

Chapter 6 Changes in ecosystems

This chapter focuses on changes in ecosystems, and begins by discussing the boundaries between ecosystems and what effect they have on the organisms that live there. Ecosystems are always changing, whether through seasonal changes, or due to natural disasters or colonisation by new organisms.

Ecosystems vary depending on distance from the equator, altitude above sea level, and many other factors. Organisms within an ecosystem can change their environment. Sometimes the changes an organism makes to its environment negatively affect the whole community.

A succession of ecosystems occurs when ecosystems transition from one type to another. A bare patch of land (due to volcanic eruption or erosion) may be colonised by grasses, which are later replaced by increasingly larger plants and trees until an equilibrium is reached. This equilibrium is called a climax community, in which there is relatively little change. The stages before this point is reached are termed seral communities, or seres.

Ecosystems of the past are discussed, as are the techniques employed to study past climates. Core samples can be taken of soil, rock or ice, with different layers corresponding to different times, giving scientists an indication of past conditions.

Finally, the human impact on biodiverse ecosystems is described in depth, and the effects of land clearing, habitat fragmentation, pollution, agricultural chemicals, waterway changes and introduced pests are discussed.

CHAPTER CHECKLIST

Read this checklist before you complete this chapter's activities then return to it to check your understanding before your assessments.

Once you have completed this chapter, you can use the 'I can …' statements to assess your understanding of the topics covered by ticking the appropriate box in the 'rating column'.

I can …	Confidently	Partially	Not really
… understand interactions between natural ecosystems			
… understand how natural communities can change			
… explain how ecosystems changed in the past and why			
… explain how humans have influenced biodiversity			

DATA DRILL 6

Reading ice core data

Ice cores are long cylinders of ice drilled from ice sheets, such as those found in Antarctica. They can be up to 3 km deep and provide climate information for the past. A 3 km ice core was extracted from the Vostok site in Antarctica before hitting bedrock. Several measurements were taken at 100 m intervals, and are shown in the graphs below.

FIGURE 1 Cutting ice cores in Antarctica

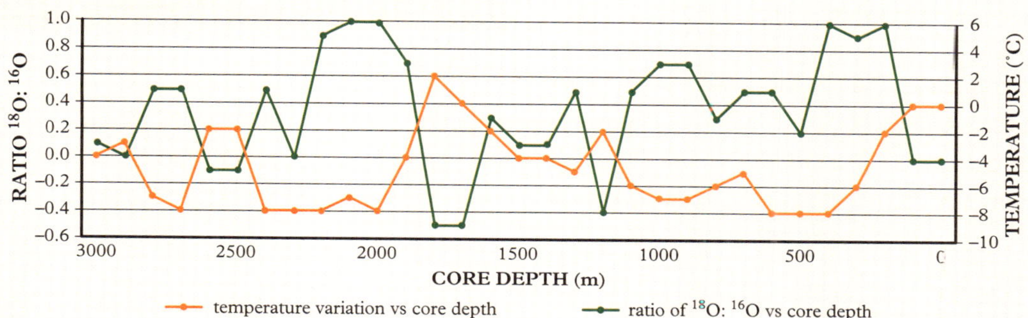

FIGURE 2 Oxygen isotope ratios alongside temperatures in the Vostok ice core

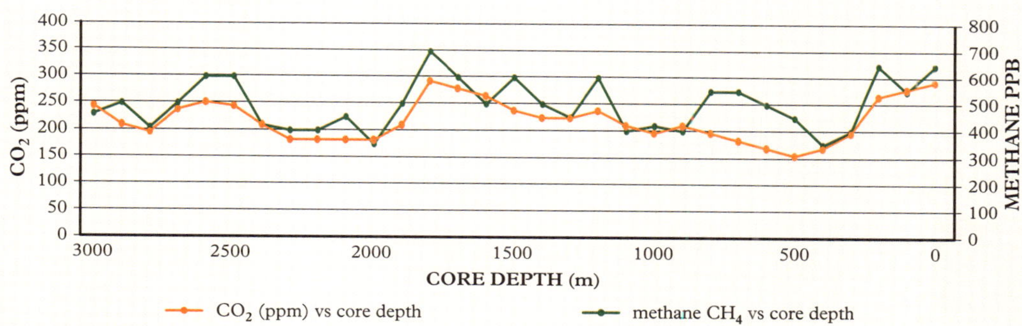

FIGURE 3 Carbon dioxide alongside methane concentrations in the Vostok ice core

1 a From Figure 2, **describe** the relationship between the ratio ^{18}O:^{16}O and the variation in temperature.

____

____

b From Figures 2 and 3, **describe** the relationship between CO_2 and temperature.

____

____

2 Methane is a potent greenhouse gas and is produced from various sources. **Determine** which other factor shown in the graphs above is also a likely cause of changes in the climate according to the ice-core data.

____

____

EXPERIMENT EXPLORER 6

Growing food for a changing world

Wheat is a staple food crop for much of the world's population. A future challenge facing scientists is how to grow wheat with increased levels of pollution, salinity, drought, wildfires, and tropical storms.

FIGURE 4 A wheat crop

1 Choose one of the following factors and **construct** a brief experimental method that could be conducted in a laboratory to test the effect the increase in this factor would have on the germination and growth of wheat plants.

- climate change
- drought
- pollution
- temperature change
- salinity
- wildfires
- tropical storms
- erosion
- soil degradation

2 Workplace Health and Safety Queensland defines hazards and risks as below.

Hazard	A situation or thing that has the potential to harm a person.
Risk	The possibility that harm (i.e. death, an injury or an illness) might occur when exposed to a hazard.

Conduct a risk assessment for your method listed above. **Use** these steps as guides for your risk assessment.

Step	Hazard 1	Hazard 2	Hazard 3
Step 1: Identify hazards. Are there any potential hazards in your method?			
Step 2: Assess the risk. What is the likelihood of this hazard causing injury, illness or death?			
Step 3: Control the risk. How can you reduce the likelihood of this hazard causing injury, illness or death?			

Step	Hazard 1	Hazard 2	Hazard 3
Step 4: Reviewing risk controls. Risk assessments are regularly reviewed to see if the controls in place are working. How would you review your controls?			

RESEARCH REVIEW 6

Rejecting or accepting a scientific claim

When analysing a scientific claim, there are a few things to consider:

- Is the source of the story credible?
- Is it based on scientific data, or is it based on opinionated, biased and anecdotal evidence?
- Does it use scientific measurements, or rely on terms like 'some', 'most of the time', 'may' and 'occasionally'?
- Are the science 'facts' agreed upon by the larger scientific community?

The editor of a science magazine was sent two new studies to review for possible publication in the next edition.

Consider the two claims below and **decide** whether the editor should accept the claims and publish the studies, or whether to reject them.

1 **Story 1**

A skin care company conducted a study on the palm oil it uses in its products. It claims that palm oil is an essential ingredient in its products, so it can't be replaced by anything else. It also claims palm oil has some antioxidant qualities, and may also have anti-cancer properties.

____

____

____

____

2 **Story 2**

A NATA-accredited testing laboratory was hired by the federal government to test the concentration of petroleum effluent in the sediments of a mangrove ecosystem following mass fish deaths in the area. The government would like to print the results in the science magazine for transparency reasons. The laboratory found that 75% of the mangrove ecosystem showed high levels of petroleum effluent, which most likely led to the fish deaths.

____

____

____

____

EXAM EXCELLENCE 6

Multiple choice – circle the correct answer

1 Where you would most likely find an animal undergoing aestivation?

A a very dry climate

B a very cold climate

C a very wet climate

D at high altitudes

2 Mangroves are facultative halophytes rather than obligate halophytes. Define the terms 'facultative' and 'obligate'.

A facultative: necessary; obligate: optional

B facultative: optional; obligate: necessary

C facultative: latitude; obligate: altitude

D facultative: pioneer species; obligate: succession species

3 Which of the following is **not** an example of primary succession?

A a forest growing on an old lava flow

B grasses sprouting in place of a retreating glacier

C plants growing on newly formed sand dunes

D seeds sprouting after a bushfire

4 Which ancient environment would have the least complete fossil record?

A marshlands

B landslides

C grasslands

D floodplains

5 Which of the following is **not** a characteristic of an urban microclimate?

A warmer than surrounding landscape

B isolated pockets of vegetation

C increased biodiversity

D presence of wind tunnels due to rows of tall buildings

Short answer

6 **a** **Define** the terms:

i primary succession

____

____

ii secondary succession.

____

____

b **Explain** why secondary succession occurs faster than primary succession.

____

____

____

7 Study the graph in Figure 5 of latitudinal zonation versus altitudinal zonation.

   a **Describe** how the vegetation changes from the equator to the poles.

   ____

   ____

   ____

   ____

   ____

   b **Infer** why altitude influences the types of vegetation in a similar way to latitude.

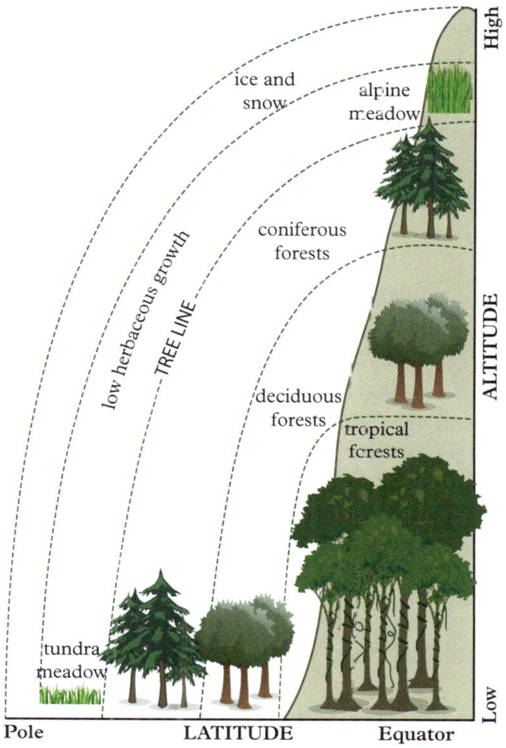

   ____

   ____

   ____

   ____

   ____

FIGURE 5 Latitudinal zonation versus altitudinal zonation

8 **Explain** the role of pollen in determining the likely climate of past ecosystems.

____

____

9 **Explain** how vegetation corridors can increase biodiversity.

____

____

10 **Sketch** a flowchart to demonstrate how excess fertiliser on farmland can lead to fish in a nearby stream dying.

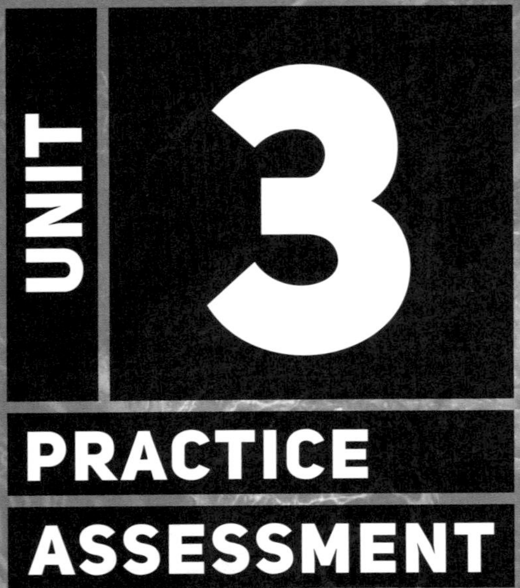

Biodiversity and the interconnectedness of life

Throughout the chapters in this unit, you have practised analysing and recording data, conducting research and modifying an experiment.

In this section, you will compete one of each of the following internal assessments:

- the Data test (10%)
- the Student experiment (20%)
- the Research investigation (20%; assessed in Unit 4).

Note: These assessments may not reflect the QCAA assessments. However, they build on the skills required for each internal assessment.

Unit 3 Data test

Dataset 1

A survey of the brown antechinus, *Antechinus stuartii*, was undertaken in the rainforest of Mt Glorious (south-east Queensland) over a period of 6 months. Two hundred traps were randomly placed in a 1 km^2 quadrat on the first weekend of each month. All new captured individuals were marked with a spot of waterproof, non-toxic paint on the back of the neck at each trapping. The experimenters recorded the gender and weight of each individual caught. The population size (N) after each trapping was calculated using the Lincoln Index

$$N = \frac{M \times n}{m}$$

where M = number of individuals marked

n = total number of individuals captured at that time

m = number of recaptured (marked) individuals.

The results of the study are shown below.

TABLE 1 Number of *Antechinus stuartii* captured over a 6-month period at Mt Glorious

	June	July		August		September		October		November	
		M		*M*		*M*		*M*		*M*	
Males											
Mean weight (g)	40		45		60		65		35		–
New	20		15		10		2		1		0
No. individuals marked (M)		20		35		45		47		48	
Recaptured (m)			10		20		25		0		0
Total caught (n)	20		25		30		27		1		0
Females											
Mean weight (g)	30		35		35		35		35		35
New	15		10		15		10		5		6*
No. individuals marked (M)		15		25		40		50		55	
Recaptured (m)			10		10		15		30		35*
Total caught (n)	15		20		25		25		35		41*
N males			50		52				0		0
N females			30		62				58		64
N total			79		66				120		120

*All females with young in pouch.

Item 1 (apply understanding)

- Calculate the population density for September of:

3 marks

a males

____

____

____

b females

____

____

____

c total individuals

Item 2 (interpret evidence)

- Using the data, draw conclusions about this population.

2 marks

Item 3 (interpret evidence)

- Infer the proportion of males and females that might be present if trapping were to be performed in the following March.

2 marks

Dataset 2

A study was made of the distribution of bell miners, *Manorina melanophrys*, around Enoggera Reservoir (in south-east Queensland). These are aggressive birds that actively drive other birds out of their area. They feed on lerps, sugary protective casings deposited by the sap-sucking psyllid insect, *Cardiaspina fiscella*. Both of the dominant eucalypts in the area (*Eucalyptus propinqua* and *E. drepanophylla*) harbour psyllids. In order to look at factors that could influence the distribution of the bell miner, 100 m × 5 m transect surveys were conducted through vegetation typical of that in which bell miners were and were not present. Both areas had the same soil type and were the same distance from the edge of the reservoir. Grasses and herbs were found throughout both transect lines. Two measures were made of the percentage of foliage cover – one by measuring the diameter of the canopy (as plotted on the diagrams below) and the other by using a cross-wire tube and recording the number of foliage sites of the trees as a percentage of the total number of observation sites.

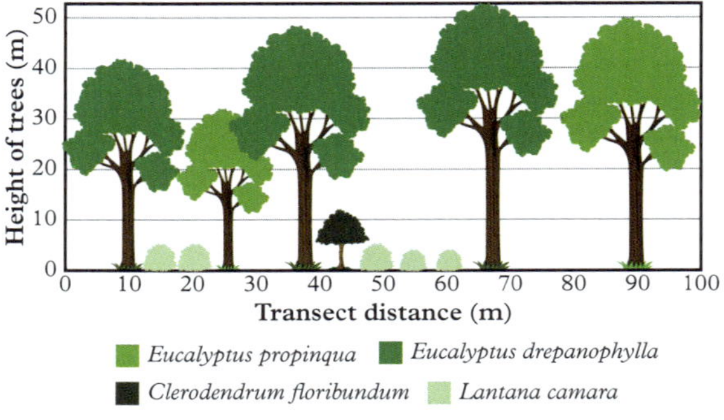

FIGURE 1 Transect A – bell miners present

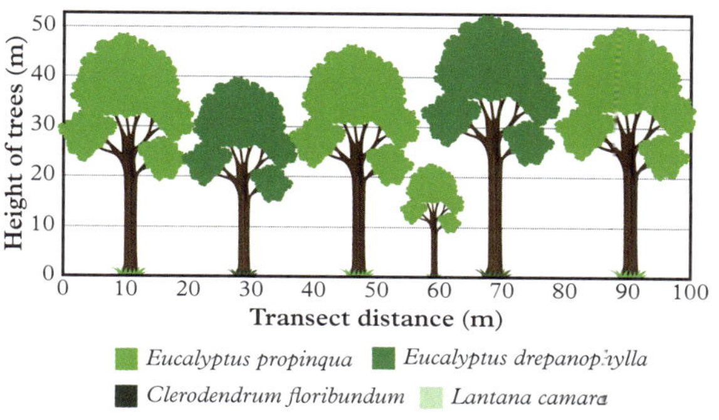

FIGURE 2 Transect B – bell miners absent

TABLE 2 Cross-wire tube recordings

Distance from start of transect (m)	Transect A	Transect B
10	Leaves	Leaves
20	Sky	Sky
30	Leaves	Leaves
40	Leaves	Sky
50	Sky	Leaves
60	Sky	Leaves
70	Sky	Sky
80	Leaves	Leaves
90	Sky	Leaves
100	Leaves	Leaves

Item 4 (apply understanding)

- Determine the percentage of foliage cover for each transect using both methods.

1 mark

Item 5 (apply understanding)

- Identify the type of trees present and, based on their leaf arrangement, determine which of the two methods for calculating percentage of foliage cover is more reliable.

2 marks

Item 6 (analyse evidence)

- Using Specht's structural classification of Australian vegetation, classify the vegetation in each transect.

1 mark

TABLE 3 Specht's structural classification of Australian vegetation

Growth form of tallest stratum	Foliage cover by the tallest stratum			
	>70%	30–70%	10–30%	<10%
Tall trees (>30 m)	Tall closed forest	Tall open forest	Tall woodland	
Medium trees (10–30 m)	Closed forest	Open forest	Woodland	Open woodland
Low trees (<10 m)	Low closed forest	Low open forest	Low woodland	Low open woodland
Tall shrubs (>2 m)	Closed scrub	Open scrub	Tall shrubland	Tall open shrubland
Low shrubs (<2 m)	Closed heath	Open heath	Low shrubland	Low open shrubland
Hummock grasses			Hummock grassland	
Tufted/tussock grasses	Closed tussock grassland	Tussock grassland	Open tussock grassland	Dense open grassland
Graminoids	Closed sedgeland	Sedgeland	Open sedgeland	
Other herbaceous species	Dense sown pasture	Sown pasture	Open herb field	Sparse open herb field

Item 7 (interpret evidence)

- Compare the vegetation of the two transects.

3 marks

Item 8 (interpret evidence)

- Deduce the distribution of bell miners around Enoggera Reservoir.

1 mark

Dataset 3

An energy flow model of a food web in a lawn ecosystem was constructed as shown below.

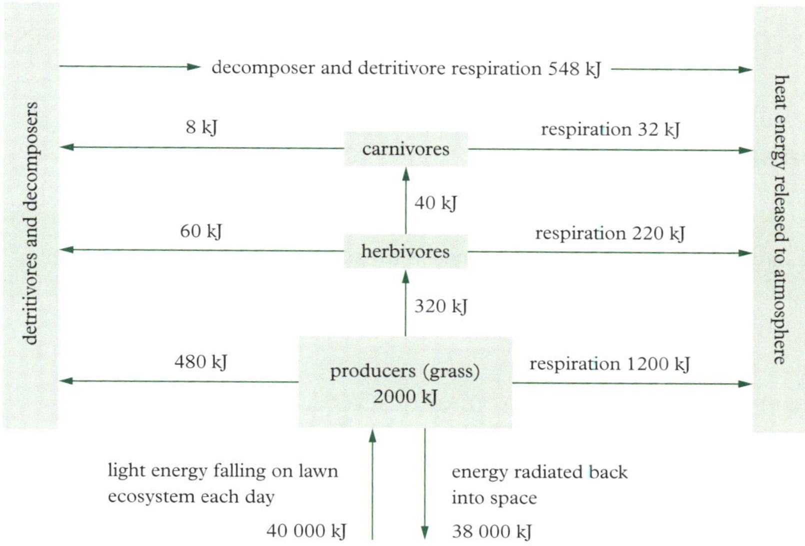

FIGURE 3 Energy flow model of a food web in a lawn ecosystem

Item 9 (interpret evidence)

- Compare, with reasons, the percentage heat loss by producers and carnivores.

4 marks

Item 10 (apply understanding)

- Calculate the percentage of solar energy converted to chemical energy that is passed on to detritivores and decomposers during photosynthesis.

1 mark

Unit 3 Student experiment

Your task is to modify the following experiment. Please note that you must conduct a risk assessment before conducting this experiment. See page 56. This is a requirement of the student experiment.

4.1B Measuring biomass

CAUTION: Heating devices can cause burns – handle with care.

Aim

To compare and contrast the wet and dry biomass of several samples of producers

Materials

- Five 27 × 35 cm Ziploc plastic bags
- Digital scales
- Paper
- Oven
- Desiccator containing a drying agent (e.g. blue silica gel)
- Baking paper

Method

1 Completely fill each bag with green leaves from five different types of plant, immediately sealing each bag once it is full. Label each bag with the plant name and the number of plants from which the material was collected (e.g. with short grasses it may take 20 plants to fill the bag, but only a couple for taller grasses, or one plant if it is a tree or shrub).

2 Weigh and record each sample.

3 Compare the wet biomass (before drying) with the number of plants from which the leaves were collected. (This is a rough comparison only, since it is unlikely that all the leaves from a shrub or tree would fit into one bag.) Also compare the wet biomass of the same volume for all the different types of species present.

4 Carefully measure 10 g of material from each plant and place the 10 g samples onto individual pieces of paper. Spread the material out as much as possible. Label each with the plant name.

5 Place the plant material in an oven at 105°C on baking paper for approximately 24 hours. When the leaves are completely dry but not charred, remove them from the oven and place in a desiccator to cool to room temperature. Reweigh each sample. Record the weight.

6 Calculate the weight of the water (wet weight or 10 g minus dry weight) and the percentage of water (weight of water ÷ fresh weight × 100) in each sample.

7 Compare the dry biomass of the different species.

Results

Plant	Wet biomass (A) in grams	Number of plants (B)	Dried biomass/10 g wet biomass (*C*)	Mass of water in leaves (10 – *C*) in grams	Percentage of water in plant (10 – *C*)/*C* × 100
Correa sp.	252	5	7.6/10	2.4	3.1%
Anigozanthos sp.	512	1	6.5/10	3.5	54%

Plant	Wet biomass (A) in grams	Number of plants (B)	Dried biomass/10 g wet biomass (*C*)	Mass of water in leaves (10 – *C*) in grams	Percentage of water in plant (10 – *C*)/*C* × 100
Eucalyptus sp.	458	1	6.8/10	3.2	47%
Lomandra sp.	1013	8	7.9/10	2.1	27%
Banksia sp.	1124	2	5.8/10	4.2	72%
Acacia sp.	882	1	7.0/10	3.0	43%

Modification of the original experiment

Note: This section provides prompts for your modification. You may require extra space to write your full practice assessment.

Aim

Research question

Background research

Methodology

Results

Discussion (rationale)

Risk assessment

Student's name: ______________________________

Experiment: ______________________________

Note: Risks should be managed by use of personal protective equipment and/or specified control measures. Always consult your teacher before conducting an experiment.

Equipment required

____

____

____

____

____

____

____

____

Hazardous chemicals required/produced

Reactant or product name and concentration	GHS classification	GHS hazard statement	Control measures

Non-hazardous substances

Reactant or product name and concentration	GHS classification	GHS hazard statement	Control measures

Other hazards and possible risks

Protective measures

Lab coat	Safety glasses	Gloves	Fume cupboard	Other

Clean up and disposal of wastes

Teacher's signature: ____________________

Student's signature: ____________________

Date: ____________

Note: This assessment is not valid until it has been completed and signed by your teacher.

Unit 3 Research investigation

Note: The Research investigation (IA3) is completed in Unit 4 and covers content from Unit 4. There is no assessable Research investigation during Unit 3. This Research investigation has been included to practice skills required for the Unit 4 assessment.

CASE STUDY

Climate change: natural or not?

Evidence of climate change has been confirmed all over the world. Earth's average surface temperature has risen by 0.9°C since the late 1800s, with records for highest temperatures being broken every year. Oceans absorb much of this extra heat, and this has led to an increase in the water temperature by 0.2°C. Ice sheets in Greenland and Antarctica have decreased in mass by 400 billion tonnes since 1993. This, combined with the increased water temperature, has seen sea levels rise by 20 cm in the last century. The acidity of the ocean's surface has increased by about 30%, leading to coral bleaching. Climate change has been linked to an increase in levels of carbon dioxide, methane and other heat-trapping greenhouse gases.

Nations around the world are responding to climate change through two processes: mitigation and adaptation.

Mitigation involves reducing those factors that have been shown to cause climate change. It is an attempt to slow down and even halt the rapid rise of temperatures that we are seeing. Some forms of mitigation include planting trees to absorb carbon from the atmosphere, reducing the release of greenhouse gases, and switching to renewable energy wherever possible.

Adaptation relies on preparing civilisation to adjust to the future climate; this can be done by changing the agricultural and industrial practices we employ, how we process and use resources like water, and the way our cities are built. Most agricultural enterprises have some form of climate change policy available to help farmers adapt to climate change.

FIGURE 1 Greenhouse gases released from industry

Your task is to conduct a Research investigation about the following claim, which is related to the case study above:

Climate change is a natural cycle of planet Earth; in fact, Earth has gone through multiple warming and cooling periods. This is just another natural spike in temperature and is not caused by humans. Mitigation isn't necessary!

Research question

Research

Note: This section provides space for you to investigate two sources; you will need to research further to complete the assessment.

Resource 1

- Title:
- Authors:
- Source and credibility:
- Publication date:
- Aim:
- Resource's research question:
- Methodology
  - What data were collected?
  - How were the data collected?

- Results
  - Did the resource support your research question?

  - Why does/doesn't it support the provided claim?

Resource 2

- Title:
- Authors:
- Source and credibility:
- Publication date:
- Aim:
- Resource's research question:
- Methodology
  - What data were collected?
  - How were the data collected?

- Results
  - Did the resource support your research question?

  - Why does/doesn't it support the provided claim?

Planning your internal assessment

UNIT 4

Heredity and continuity of life

PRACTICALS IN THIS UNIT

	SUGGESTED PRACTICAL	**7.1** Extraction of DNA from strawberries
	SUGGESTED PRACTICAL	**12.2** Bacterial transformations
	SUGGESTED PRACTICAL	**12.4** Gel electrophoresis
	MANDATORY PRACTICAL	**14.3** Changes in the gene pool due to selection pressure

WORD WIZARD

Draw a line to match each term with the correct definition.

DEOXYRIBONUCLEIC ACID (DNA)	An organic compound comprising only carbon and hydrogen atoms
HYDROCARBON	A thread-like chain of nucleotides carrying the genetic instructions in a double-helix of antiparallel strands
REDOX	A nitrogen fixation process to produce ammonia
REDUCTION	A gain in electrons from an atom from another atom
GENE	A region of DNA, made up of nucleotides, that encodes a function
HALF-CELL	A chemical reaction involving the transfer of electrons from one reactant to another
RIBONUCLEIC ACID (RNA)	The atomically precise placement of atoms or molecules in order to build larger molecular assemblies or molecular-based machines
OXIDATION	A loss of electron from one atom to another
DNA LIGASE	Contains either the oxidation or reduction redox reaction
KETONE	A thread-like chain of nucleotides carrying the genetic instructions to form a protein in a cell
POLYSACCHARIDE	Organisms able to breakdown a substance, such as plastic
AMINO ACID	An organic compound comprising an amine and a carboxyl functional group
MASS SPECTROMETRY	An enzyme that joins pieces of DNA
HABER PROCESS	A technique used to determine the molecular weight of a compound
BIODEGRADATION	A class of organic compound that contains a carbonyl functional group in the middle of the main chain
MOLECULAR MANUFACTURING	A molecular system with a defined energy input that is capable of performing a useful function at the nanoscale
MOLECULAR MACHINE	Multiple sugar monomers bonded together
MITOSIS	Nuclear division resulting in daughter cells having the same number and type of chromosomes as the parent cell
Y CHROMOSOME	Male sex chromosome in vertebrates and some other animals
MUTATION	Small permanent change in the DNA of an organism
KARYOTYPE	The number and visual appearance of the chromosomes in the cell nuclei of an organism or species

CHAPTER 7

DNA structure and replication

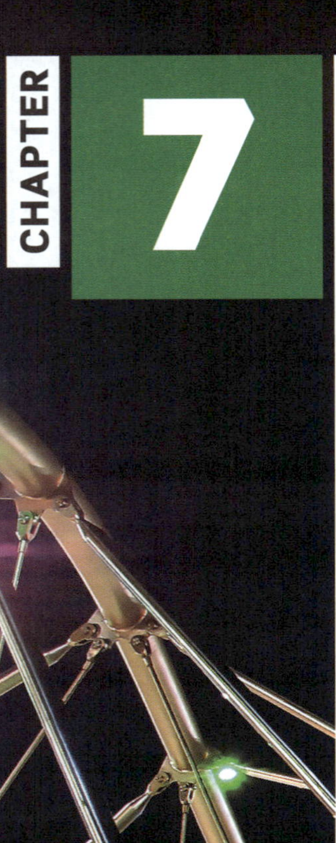

This chapter focuses on the structure of deoxyribonucleic acid (DNA), long considered the blueprint of life. DNA occurs in the nucleus of eukaryotes, in the cytoplasm of prokaryotes, and in two distinct and interesting cellular organelles: mitochondria and chloroplasts.

DNA is a helical molecule, made of a phosphate–sugar backbone connected to an antiparallel strand via nitrogen bases. The four nitrogen bases (adenine, guanine, cytosine and thymine [and its RNA equivalent uracil]), their hydrogen bonding and their complementary nature are explored.

The different types of ribonucleic acid (RNA) – transfer RNA, messenger RNA and ribosomal RNA – are mentioned briefly, to be discussed in depth further on in the unit. The role of two essential enzymes, helicase and DNA polymerase, are explored in relation to DNA replication and the multiple stages involved, including initiation of replication, elongation and termination.

Finally, the controversial discovery of the double-helix nature of DNA by Franklin, Wilkins, Watson and Crick is described. This discovery led to a better understanding of DNA and paved the way for modern genetic techniques.

CHAPTER CHECKLIST

Read this checklist before you complete this chapter's activities and then return to it to check your understanding before your assessments.

Once you have completed this chapter, you can use the 'I can …' statements to assess your understanding of the topics covered by ticking the appropriate box in the 'rating column'.

I can …	Confidently	Partially	Not really
… explain the chemical structure of nuclei acids			
… explain the chemical structure of DNA			
… understand how DNA gets replicated			

RESEARCH REVIEW 7

Using scientific language correctly

As we learn about science throughout our school years, we are introduced to complicated concepts that are simplified to our current level of learning. In Year 7, we learn about physics in a simple way, using analogies of car crashes to understand force and motion. As we work with cells in Year 8, we are told that the nucleus is the brain of the cell. During Year 9, atoms are presented as being made of protons, neutrons and electrons, not quarks and bosons. As part of your Unit 4 assessments, you will need to understand and define specific biological terms.

1 'Biology' is an all-encompassing term that refers to any scientific study of life and its origins. **Define** the following areas of biology.

   a Neurobiology

   ____

   ____

   b Entomology

   ____

   ____

   c Virology

   ____

   ____

   d Epigenetics

   ____

   ____

2 As science advances, some areas of science are superseded by newer theories. **Define** the following now debunked terms:

   a spontaneous generation

   ____

   ____

   b phrenology

   ____

   ____

   c homunculus

   ____

   ____

FIGURE 1 The Millaa Millaa Rainforest in North Queensland is under the *Environment Protection and Biodiversity Conservation Act 1999* due to its large number of rare and endangered animals.

Study tip

At senior biology levels, it is time to upgrade our terminology: structure and function, for instance, becomes anatomy and physiology.

EXAM EXCELLENCE 7

Multiple choice – circle the correct answer

1 Identify the correct structure of a nucleotide.

A
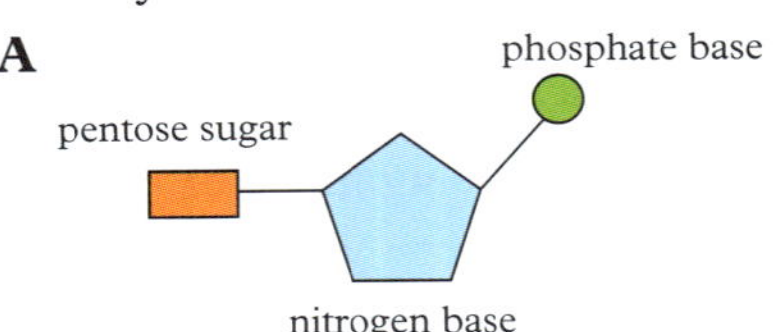

B
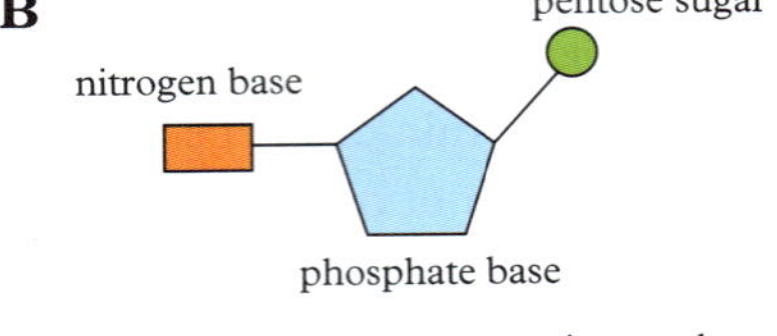

C
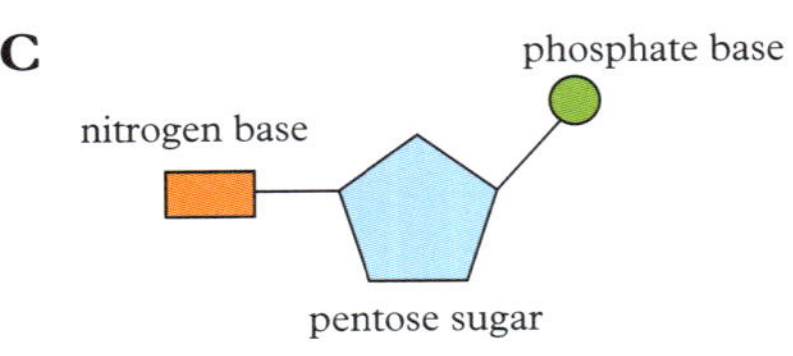

D
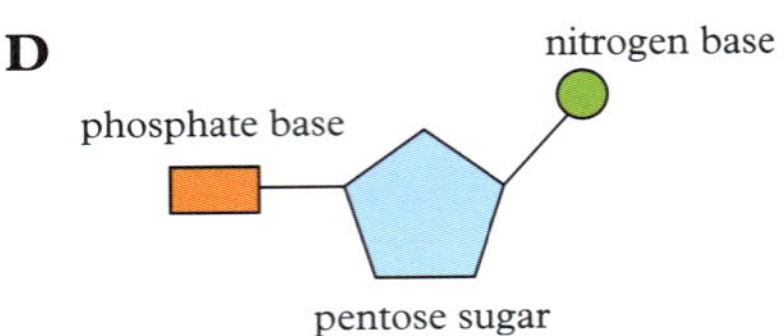

2 In order for a double-helix molecule of DNA to form,

A each strand of the molecule must strongly bond with another strand

B the complimentary strands must twist upon themselves

C single-stranded DNA must link with another DNA molecule

D the two strands of the molecule must be anti-parallel prior to coiling

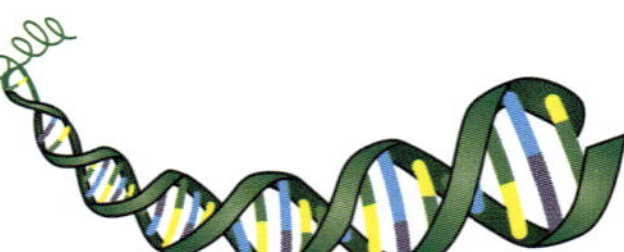

FIGURE 2 The double helix structure of DNA

3 Which of the following is not a characteristic of prokaryote DNA?

A DNA arranged in chromosomes

B no presence of histone

C DNA found in cytoplasm

D circular DNA

4 The field of epigenetics is a relatively new and exciting area of biology. Epigenetic factors have been found to influence the expression of genes in various ways. Some types of epigenetic factors control the replication of DNA by binding to the tails of a histone protein. How do these epigenetic factors affect DNA replication?

A by accelerating the unwinding of DNA

B by inhibiting the unwinding of DNA

C by binding to DNA and 'unzipping' it

D by repairing DNA mutations during replication

5 Which DNA enzyme is the last to interact with Okazaki fragments?

A helicase

B polymerase

C ligase

D histone

Short answer

6 **Contrast** the structure and function of eukaryote DNA and RNA in the table below.

	DNA	RNA
Structure		
Function		

7 **Determine** the code of the complementary DNA strand and the code of the complementary mRNA strand for the following sequence.

DNA strand	ATGGTTTATTCCTCCCGCTTCAAAAACCGTCGATCGCTAGCATAA
Complementary DNA strand	
mRNA strand	

8 **Describe** the relationship between the following.

a histones and nucleosomes ______________________________

____

b thymine and uracil ______________________________

____

9 **Identify** the correct phrase, by circling the correct word(s), to complete these sentences.

a (All/Not all) enzymes are proteins, but (all/not all) proteins are enzymes.

b The (lagging/leading) strand is replicated towards the replication fork, and the (lagging/leading) strand is replicated away from the replication fork.

10 **Construct** a flowchart of DNA replication of the lagging strand.

Cellular replication and variation

This chapter compares the two forms of cellular replication found in eukaryotes: meiosis and mitosis. Meiosis occurs in the sex cells through the process of gametogenesis (the generation of gametes), which can further be divided into spermatogenesis (in males) and oogenesis (in females), and it results in haploid cells.

'Haploid' and 'diploid' cells refer to the number of chromosomes present. In humans, haploid gamete cells (containing one copy of each chromosome) from a male and a female combine to produce a diploid cell, which can then develop into an embryo. The law of segregation and the law of independent assortment help to explain how chromosomes and genes are passed from parent to child.

'Diploid' refers to those somatic cells, the body cells, that contain two sets of each chromosome. The process by which they multiply is called mitosis, which was discussed in depth in Unit 1 and should be reviewed as part of this unit.

In a 'Science as a Human Endeavour' spread, the role of genetic screening of embryos is discussed, including that occurring pre-implantation of the embryo, and that employed during pregnancy. An introduction to the newly developed CRISPR technique is explored, together with a discussion of its potential uses, which are still being discovered.

CHAPTER CHECKLIST

Read this checklist before you complete this chapter's activities and then return to it to check your understanding before your assessments.

Once you have completed this chapter, you can use the 'I can …' statements to assess your understanding of the topics covered by ticking the appropriate box in the 'rating column'.

I can …	Confidently	Partially	Not really
… explain cell division and replication processes			
… define gametogenesis			
… understand the difference between genes and alleles			

RESEARCH REVIEW 8

Using the right images in a scientific report

Images from the internet are often used in scientific reports, posters and textbooks as a visual aid to explain a concept in science.

1 View the following images, involving genetic modification and syringes, and **research** what they are representing, and why they would not be scientifically accurate. **Consider** alternative figures for each image.

  a Image 1

FIGURE 1 Image 1 showing genetic modification

  b Image 2

FIGURE 2 Image 2 showing genetic modification

EXAM EXCELLENCE 8

Multiple choice – circle the correct answer

1 Which acronym represents the steps of meiosis?

A IPMAT

B IMPATC I(II) M(II) P (II) A(II) T(II) C(II)

C IPMAT I(II) P(II) M (II) A(II) T(II)

D IPMATC I(II) P(II) M (II) A(II) T(II) C(II)

2 Complete the following sentence.

__________ occurs in the gonads. ___________ is the formation of __________ cells in the testes. ___________ is the formation of ova in the __________.

A Spermatogenesis; Oogenesis; sperm; Gametogenesis; ovaries.

B Gametogenesis; Spermatogenesis; ova; Oogenesis; ovaries.

C Gametogenesis; Oogenesis; ova; Spermatogenesis; testes.

D Gametogenesis; Spermatogenesis; sperm; Oogenesis; ovaries.

3 In conifers, there are 24 chromosomes in each autosomal cell. **Determine** the number of chromosomes in a pollen grain.

A 24

B 48

C 12

D 96

4 An autosome

A forms the centromere

B is a non-sex-determining chromosome

C is a chromosome involved in sex determination

D is a replicated chromosome

5 The chromosome condition found in the body cells of sexually reproducing animals is

A diploid

B haploid

C tetraploid

D anaploid

Short answer

6 **Sketch** and label the following stages of meiosis in the boxes below.

Anaphase I	Metaphase II	Telophase II

7 **Consider** the human karyotype to the right. **Determine** whether these cells are diploid or haploid.

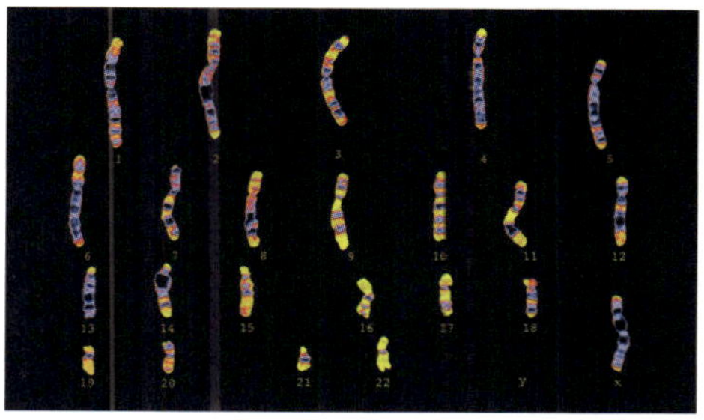

FIGURE 3 Human karyotype

8 Polycystic ovarian syndrome (PCOS) is a complicated condition that affects 12–18% of all women of child-bearing age. In PCOS, abnormal hormone levels prevent follicles from growing and maturing to release ova. The follicles form cysts, and can be seen on ultrasound as a series of dark circles. **Determine** at which stage of oogenesis follicular cysts would form.

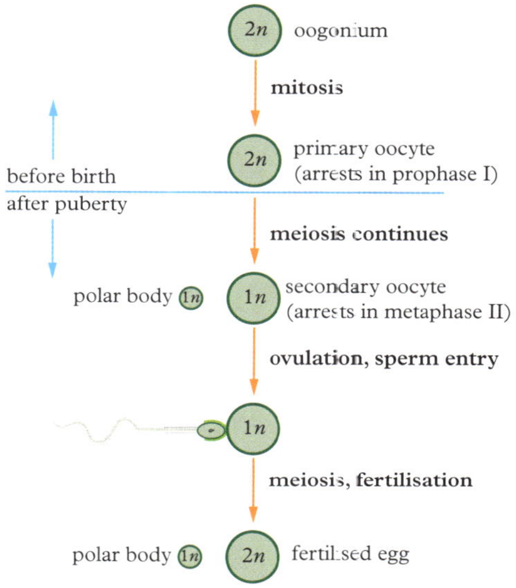

FIGURE 4 Oogenesis showing the cell types and divisions involved

9 **Compare** the following terms.

a genotype and phenotype

b recessive trait and dominant trait

10 **Explain** why the following cross-over event is unlikely to occur.

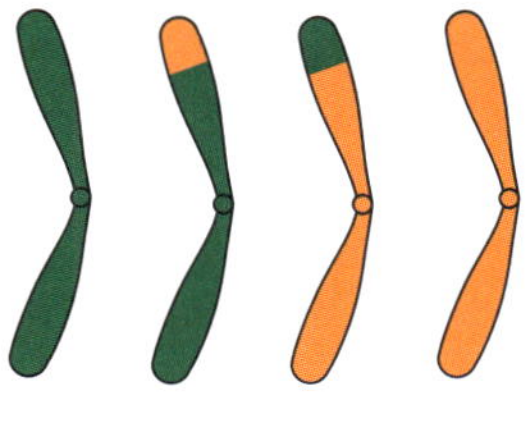

FIGURE 5 Gametes

Gene expression

This chapter begins by defining a genome as the sum of all the genetic material found in the chromosomes of an organism. Non-coding regions of the genome are those that do not code for a protein, such as telomeres, centromeres and the different types of RNA molecules. The concept of structural genes that are controlled by regulatory genes is explained.

One of the most important concepts in genetics, that of the triplet codon, is introduced at this stage. Triplet codons determine where DNA transcription begins (start codons) and where it ends (stop codons). During protein assembly, they determine which amino acids are translated by the different RNA types, and even the shape and function of the protein produced. Transcription and translation are two steps necessary in the manufacturing of proteins, and the triplet codon is essential to both.

Gene expression refers to whether the genes in a particular cell are either 'switched on' and are being expressed, or 'switched off' and not being expressed. This is an important part of cell differentiation. Gene expression can be regulated during transcription, post-transcription, and during translation into polypeptides.

Epigenetics is discussed and defined as a set of internal and external factors that can influence which part of the DNA is expressed. External factors can include exercise, diet, health, medications and the psychological effects on gene expression. Twin studies are very useful in learning about epigenetics.

To conclude this chapter, homeotic genes (which relate to anatomical structures) and the role of the *SRY* gene (in determining the sex of offspring) are discussed.

CHAPTER CHECKLIST

Read this checklist before you complete this chapter's activities and then return to it to check your understanding before your assessments.

Once you have completed this chapter, you can use the 'I can …' statements to assess your understanding of the topics covered by ticking the appropriate box in the 'rating column'.

I can …	Confidently	Partially	Not really
… explain protein synthesis			
… explain the different ways of regulating a gene			
… understand the different transcription factors that are significant in development			

RESEARCH REVIEW 9

Reading abstracts

Reading a piece of scientific literature and then rewriting it in your own words demonstrates an understanding of what is said. It lends credibility to your thoughts on the matter and also negates any chance of plagiarism. The terminology can often be confusing, so it is important to decipher what is being said before analysing it further.

Break down a sentence into individual words and phrases instead of trying to understand large blocks of text. Then replace the phrases with ones you do understand. Look up any words you don't understand.

Consider the following abstract.

The use of hydrogen peroxide and acetic acid to initiate plant defence against *Phytophthora cinnamomi* in *Allium cepa*

Phytophthora cinnamomi, a soil-borne oomycete, causes widespread disease in agricultural crops and native bushland in Australia. The disease, often called cinnamon fungus, jarrah root rot or avocado root rot, is caused when the zoospores of *Phytophthora* penetrate the feeding roots of their host plant, colonise the plant xylem, and hinder transport of water and nutrients into the aerial organs. Plants that recognise the pathogen cells begin defensive measures, such as the production of phytoalexins, or an oxidative burst resulting in the formation of hydrogen peroxide H_2O_2. Hydrogen peroxide cross-links structural proteins in the cell walls of the host plant and may also play a direct part in damaging the pathogen cell. It also signals the cell to express genes relating to defence. We applied concentration of 1000 ppm of a combination of hydrogen peroxide (at 30% concentration) and acetic acid (a known antiseptic at 100% concentration) to onion plants (*Allium cepa*) prior to infection with *Phytophthora cinnamomi* 3 days later. Measurements a week after infection showed reduction in plant damage, compared with controls, indicating that either structural proteins in the walls of the onion cells had been cross-linked, or that hydrogen peroxide and acetic acid had worked directly on the pathogen in the soil.

1 Circle any terms you don't understand, research them further and **define** them below.

2 **Summarise** the method and results for this experiment using dot points.

-
-
-
-
-
-

3 **Construct** a research question that could follow from the results of this experiment.

EXAM EXCELLENCE 9

Multiple choice – circle the correct answer

1 Which of the following statements is incorrect?

A Translation occurs in the cytosol of prokaryotes and eukaryotes.

B Transcription occurs in the nucleus of eukaryotes.

C Translation involves ribosomes.

D Transcription involves tRNA.

2 Which mRNA code could have coded for the following protein: Met-Ser-Leu-Phe-Lys-Val-Stop?

A AUG-UCU-UUG-UUU-AAA-GUA-UAG

B AUC-UCU-UUG-UUU-AAA-GUA-UAA

C AUG-UGU-UUG-UUU-AAA-GUA-UAG

D AUG-UCU-UUG-UUU-AAA-GUA-UAC

3 Non-coding DNA can block the trimming, capping and tailing of mRNA, leaving it vulnerable to degradation by enzymes. This controls the amount of protein produced. Identify what kind of control this would be.

A pre-transcriptional control

B post-transcriptional control

C translational control

D epigenetic control

4 *HOX* genes are highly conserved between species. Determine what 'highly conserved' refers to in this instance.

A a group of genes that has a high mutation rate, and therefore is vastly different between species

B a group of genes only found on the X and Y chromosomes

C a group of genes consisting of very few introns.

D a group of genes that has remained relatively unchanged through the evolution of different species

5 At which stage in foetal development is the *SRY* gene transcribed to produce the Y protein?

A during birth

B after 9–12 weeks

C before 6–8 weeks

D before conception

Short answer

6 **a** **Identify** at which event mRNA is created.

____

____

b **Identify** at which event mRNA, tRNA and rRNA interact.

____

____

____

7 **Determine** the amino acid sequence of the following DNA code.
TAC-TAT-AGT-ATG-ACG-ACG-CGG-ACT

8 a There are two forms of chromatin. **Explain** why it is beneficial to have DNA in the form of euchromatin for DNA that is regularly transcribed.

b **Discuss** whether it would be more likely for the genes involved in the development of the placenta to be bound in a heterochromatin form or a euchromatin form.

9 **Define** the term 'epigenetics'.

10 Overexpressed growth-promoting genes (called oncogenes) can cause cancers of the stomach, colon and kidneys. **Discuss** how our new understanding of the epigenome could be used to treat diseases such as cancer.

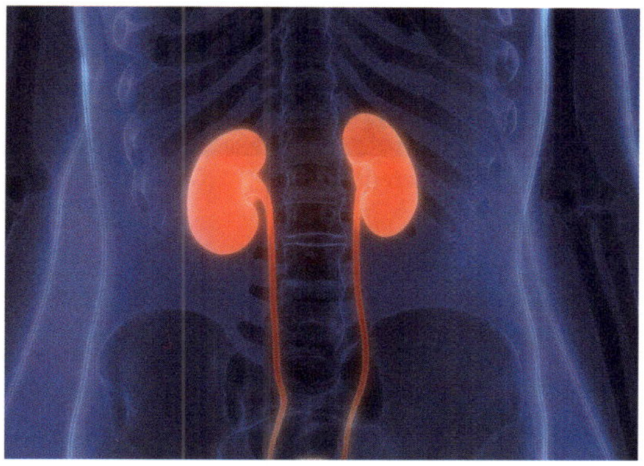

FIGURE 1 In the future, cancers of particular organs, such as the kidneys, could be targeted through epigenetics.

CHAPTER 10

Mutation

This chapter focuses on mutations in DNA, and begins by discussing those specialised proteins, such as BRCA1 and 2, that repair mutations in the DNA. When there is a mutation in the genes that code for the BRCA proteins, they can no longer repair other mutations.

Different types of mutations are explored, such as point mutations, which involve the swapping of individual nucleotides. Silent point mutations, missense point mutations, and nonsense point mutations are discussed. Frameshift mutations, with the addition or loss of a single nucleotide, cause many triplet codons to change, which in turn would alter the amino acid sequence of any protein that the gene coded for.

Genetic disorders, such as cystic fibrosis, Cri-du-chat syndrome and Down syndrome, are discussed from a genetic point of view, to highlight the effects of genome mutations on an organism. Block mutations involve a change to a large group of genes located on the same chromosome, as seen in Cri-du-chat syndrome, whereas Down syndrome arises from the presence of an additional copy of chromosome 21, and is an example of aneuploidy, meaning there is an abnormal number of chromosomes present. Missing or additional sex chromosomes also cause a range of genetic disorders, some of which are explored.

Finally, some of the causes and effects of mutations are explained, by exploring mutagens and the ways they interact with DNA. Whether the mutation is hereditary or somatic determines whether it can be passed on to the offspring. Examples of mutagens include radiation, carcinogenic chemicals, and viruses.

CHAPTER CHECKLIST

Read this checklist before you complete this chapter's activities and then return to it to check your understanding before your assessments.

Once you have completed this chapter, you can use the 'I can …' statements to assess your understanding of the topics covered by ticking the appropriate box in the 'rating column'.

I can …	Confidently	Partially	Not really
… explain the different genetic mutations			
… explain the different chromosome mutations			
… understand the different causes and effects of mutations			

RESEARCH REVIEW 10

Model organisms in research

Model organisms are those non-human species with desirable characteristics that are used extensively in laboratory studies. Often they are small organisms, with a simple, fully sequenced genome and a short generation time that are easy to breed in the laboratory. There are three types of model organisms used in research: genomic, genetic and experimental.

Those species that are used in genetic analysis include *Drosophila melanogaster* (fruit fly), *Saccharomyces cerevisiae* (baker's yeast) and *Caenorhabditis elegans* (nematode worm). Processes like transcription, replication and the effects of mutations can be studied in fruit flies to help us understand these processes in other organisms, including humans.

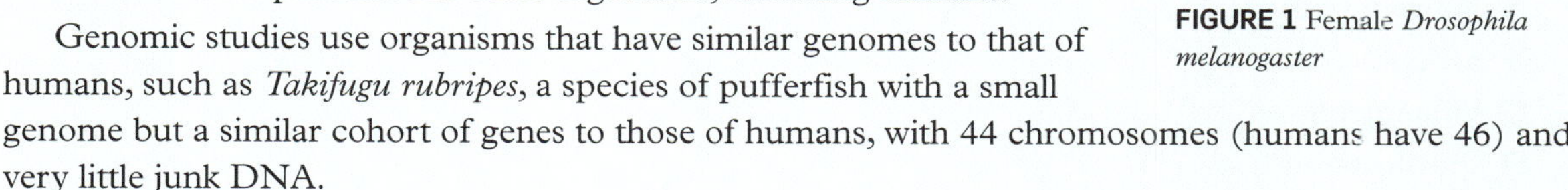

FIGURE 1 Female *Drosophila melanogaster*

Genomic studies use organisms that have similar genomes to that of humans, such as *Takifugu rubripes*, a species of pufferfish with a small genome but a similar cohort of genes to those of humans, with 44 chromosomes (humans have 46) and very little junk DNA.

Experimental model organisms may not have strong genetic links to humans, but are useful for demonstrating large processes like those involved in the development of embryos. Chickens (*Gallus domesticus*) and zebrafish (*Danio rerio*) are both suitable for this type of research.

1 **Determine** which type of organism – genomic, genetic or experimental – would be most suitable for the following studies.

   a A new genetic disease has been found in humans. Geneticists wish to study the genes involved in this disease using organisms with similar karyotypes to humans.

   b Biologists wish to view, in detail, the process involved in embryonic development in order to treat women with fertility problems.

2 **Research** online to **determine** the scientific use of the model organisms *Arabidopsis thaliana* and *Escherichia coli*.

EXAM EXCELLENCE 10

Multiple choice – circle the correct answer

1 Determine the type of point mutation in the DNA code below.

Original code	TACATGTTGTGCCAAATT
Altered code	TACATGTTCTGCCAAATT

A silent point mutation
B missense point mutation
C nonsense point mutation
D frameshift mutation

2 Which is not an example of a mutagen that occurs in everyday life?

A ionising radiation
B asbestos poisoning
C viral infection
D translocation

3 A segment of DNA undergoes a block mutation, in which the segment is turned back to front and reintegrated into the chromosome. Determine what type of block mutation this is an example of.

A deletion
B duplication
C inversion
D translocation

4 Determine what role the drug colchicine has in preparing a karyotype.

A Colchicine preserves the chromosomes so they don't degrade during analysis.
B Colchicine dyes the chromosomes, allowing them to be seen more clearly.
C Colchicine prevents anaphase from occurring, allowing chromosomes to be viewed.
D Colchicine dissolves the centromere, so the length of chromosomes can be measured.

5 Atomic gardening began in the 1950s, when agricultural scientists experimented with using radiation to produce mutations in plants to develop new varieties with desirable traits. Ruby-red grapefruits arose from these trials. Determine which of the following this was an example of.

A physical mutagen
B chemical mutagen
C biological agent
D heavy metal mutagen

Short answer

6 **Explain** how a mutated *BRCA1* gene could increase the changes of an organism developing cancer.

7 **Determine** either the genetic disease name or its cause and fill in the blanks in the table below.

Genetic disease	Cause
Sickle cell anaemia	
	An extra X chromosome in a male (XXY)
Cri-du-chat syndrome	
	Trisomy of chromosome 18
Turner's syndrome	
	Frameshift mutation of *CFTR* gene

8 **Explain** why a male with the fragile X mutation is more likely to exhibit symptoms of the condition than a female.

9 Ultraviolet radiation from the sun can result in sunburn and skin cancers such as melanoma. The UV photon causes two nitrogenous bases next to each other to bind together, forming a pyrimidine dimer.

a **Identify** three normal cell functions that a pyrimidine dimer could affect.

b Pyrimidine dimers are repaired by DNA glycosylase, a family of enzymes that remove the damaged nitrogenous bases while leaving the sugar phosphate backbone intact. **Explain** why someone who spends a lot of time outdoors is in greater danger of developing skin cancers.

10 **Compare** the terms 'mutagen' and 'carcinogen'.

CHAPTER 11

Inheritance

This chapter on inheritance introduces the concept of the allele, an alternative expression of a gene. A single individual can carry two copies of the same gene, one on each homologous chromosome. Two alleles that are the same are homozygous, and two alleles that are different are heterozygous.

The concepts of genotype and phenotype are discussed, with the genotype being the alleles that are present in an organism's genome, and the phenotype depending on which alleles are expressed and observable in the organism. In addition, the concept of dominant and recessive traits, referring to which allele is expressed in the presence of its counterpart allele, is explored.

Punnett squares are presented as a useful tool for predicting the genotypes and phenotypes of offspring. If the alleles of the parents are known, the probability of any offspring inheriting a particular allele can be calculated. This is a key concept in genetic studies.

Non-Mendelian genetics, however, suggests that the expression of alleles is not as straightforward as the dominant–recessive concept. Modifier genes and environmental transcription factors influence which alleles are expressed. Other forms of dominance are introduced, such as codominance, intermediate dominance, and poly alleles. Blood type is given as an example of poly allele inheritance.

Finally, sex-linked inheritance is explained through the examples of the disorders haemophilia and colour blindness.

CHAPTER CHECKLIST

Read this checklist before you complete this chapter's activities and then return to it to check your understanding before your assessments.

Once you have completed this chapter, you can use the 'I can …' statements to assess your understanding of the topics covered by ticking the appropriate box in the 'rating column'.

I can …	Confidently	Partially	Not really
… create Punnett squares and frequency histograms			
… explain the different non-Mendelian genetics (codominance, intermediate dominance, multiple alleles, continuous variation and gene interactions)			
… explain sex-linked inheritance			

RESEARCH REVIEW 11

Designing a poster

Creating a scientific poster as an assessment task is a great way to be concise about your research. These are a few guidelines to follow when creating a scientific poster.

- Less text – don't overcrowd your poster with text, as it can be difficult to read.
- Bullet points – use bullet points to break down large bodies of text into more manageable portions.
- Pictures and diagrams – why write about it when you can explain it through pictures and diagrams?
- Left to right/top to bottom – people read from left to right and from top to bottom, so create your poster from introduction to conclusion in this way.
- Rainbow effect – don't use too many colours; three or four contrasting colours should be enough.
- Summarise – a neat, short summary at the end can draw your reader to the rest of your work.
- Titles – keep titles short and eye-catching.

In this chapter, an explanation of blood types, including the ABO system and the rhesus protein, is given.

Use this information and the guidelines above to draft of a poster you would present on blood types and inheritance. Brainstorm your content on the lines below and draft the layout in the box provided.

EXAM EXCELLENCE 11

Multiple choice – circle the correct answer

1 Define an allele.

A two different genes

B an alternative form of a gene

C an alternative form of a protein

D a trait that is inherited

2 Identify the maximum number of alleles an organism can have.

A 1

B 2

C 23

D 46

3 An organism has the genotype *dd* for a particular trait. **Identify** the allele type.

A homozygous dominant

B heterozygous dominant

C homozygous recessive

D heterozygous recessive

4 Determine the genotype and phenotype ratios from the following Punnett square. (B = black, b = white)

A genotype: 50% homozygous dominant, 50% heterozygous; phenotype: all black

B genotype: 100% homozygous dominant; phenotype: all black

C genotype: 50% homozygous dominant, 50% heterozygous; phenotype: all white

D genotype: 50% homozygous dominant, 50% heterozygous; phenotype: 50% black, 50% white

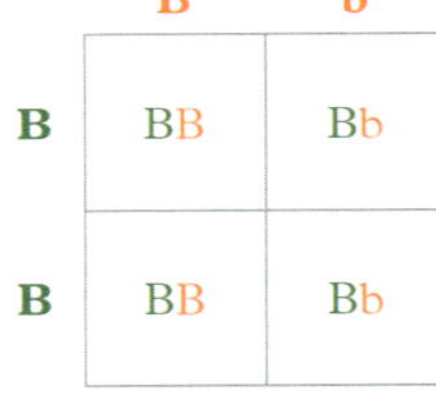

	B	b
B	BB	Bb
B	BB	Bb

FIGURE 1 Punnett square

5 Determine the type of dominance shown in the colour of the rose.

A Codominance

B Recessive

C Intermediate dominance

D Partial dominance

FIGURE 2 Multicoloured rose

Short answer

6 Gregor Mendel was an Augustinian abbot and scientist, and is considered the father of modern genetics. He experimented with breeding pea plants and found examples of simple dominant and recessive traits, such as flower colour and plant height. He went on to publish his work *Versuche über Pflanzenhybriden* (*Experiments on Plant Hybridization*), which is now considered a seminal work in genetics.

a **Define** what is meant by non-Mendelian genetics.

b **Infer** what might have happened had Mendel observed codominance or poly allele traits during his studies.

---

7 A man who is heterozygous for blood type A (I^A allele and i allele) fathers a child with a woman who is heterozygous AB (I^A and I^B alleles). **Calculate** the possible genotypes of any offspring.

8 In cattle, black colouring is dominant to red colouring, and both are codominant with white, producing roan (red × white) or grey (black × white) offspring. **Construct** a Punnett square of a red bull mated to a grey cow. **Calculate** the percentage chance that a black calf will be born.

9 Biology students' heights were measured (in centimetres): 168, 145, 155, 138, 147, 135, 152, 154, 140, 144, 148, 154, 178, 153, 141, 157, 159, 168, 151, 147, 156, 161, 164, 162, 171.

Explain why this would be an example of continuous variation by polygenic inheritance.

---

10 A geneticist breeding *Drosophila* wants to produce a white-eyed female from red-eyed females (homozygous) and white-eyed males. **Identify** a way to produce a white-eyed female from the least possible crosses, using only F1 and F2 offspring from the original parents (flies can only be crossed within the same generation). (**Hint**: This will take multiple Punnett squares to work out.)

CHAPTER 12

Biotechnology

This chapter defines biotechnology as the application of biological knowledge to the production of organisms or their products useful to humankind, which includes not just modern genetic engineering but also artificial selection and breeding strategies for desirable organisms. The latter techniques have been used for thousands of years.

The use of microorganisms to produce food such as cheese, yoghurt and bread, to decompose wastes, and to produce medicines and antibiotics is explored in depth. In addition, the discovery of the restriction enzymes found in microorganisms and the use of bacterial plasmids to clone eukaryote genes are discussed, highlighting the important part microorganisms play in biotechnology.

The cloning techniques employed to clone sheep and macaque monkeys are described as a case study. Other tools and techniques useful in genetic engineering, such as DNA ligase, which acts like a glue to assist in reattaching cut ends of DNA, and reverse transcriptase, used to transcribe mRNA back into DNA to identify the introns in the original organism's genome, are introduced,

Assessing the success of a DNA recombination process can be done using a number of techniques, such as inserting a gene for resistance to antibiotics and then growing the recombinant bacteria on an agar plate embedded with antibiotics, or inserting a gene for a blue or fluorescent pigment, which would show up in an organism whose DNA has successfully been recombined.

CHAPTER CHECKLIST

Read this checklist before you complete this chapter's activities and then return to it to check your understanding before your assessments.

Once you have completed this chapter, you can use the 'I can …' statements to assess your understanding of the topics covered by ticking the appropriate box in the 'rating column'.

I can …	Confidently	Partially	Not really
… describe the term biotechnology			
… explain the genetic engineering toolbox			
… explain the process of PCR			
… explain the Sanger sequencing method			

RESEARCH REVIEW 12

Exploring the BLAST website

BLAST (Basic Local Alignment Search Tool) is a global collection of DNA, RNA and amino acid sequences stored online and available for anyone to explore. With DNA sequences comprising millions of combinations of nucleotide bases, being able to insert sequences straight from a DNA sequencer into the BLAST tool is highly efficient.

Visit the BLAST website (https://blast.ncbi.nlm.nih.gov) and answer the follow questions.

1 Select Nucleotide BLAST. Enter the following nucleotide bases to **determine** the gene and the organism this sequence is found in (make sure the organism field is empty). Click BLAST. The gene is often difficult to identify and commonly expressed in brackets in the BLAST database.
TTCAATAGACAAGTTTAAAAACCATACCATATAACAATATATCATGGTTATCCAAAGG
AATAGTATTCTC

2 **Research** and **discuss** the link between this gene and a genetically modified organism: the FLAVR SAVR.

3 The BLAST tool is used by geneticists and researchers across the world. **Comment** on the credibility of this resource.

FIGURE 1 DNA sequence

EXAM EXCELLENCE 12

Multiple choice – circle the correct answer

1 Identify which of the following is **not** considered biotechnology.

A cloning

B selective plant breeding

C food processing with microorganisms

D natural selection

2 Cloning:

A only refers to the production of an identical organism from an adult cell

B is the production of genetically similar organisms, cells or tissues

C is the only means of producing crop uniformity in plants

D always involves the use of somatic cell nuclear transfer

3 Identify which restriction enzyme you would use to cut the following DNA sequence.
ATCCTGCAGAGCTGGAGC

A *Eco* RI

B *Hpa* I

C *Sst* I

D *Pst* I

4 Identify which type of cell would **not** be suitable for somatic gene therapy.

A red blood cell

B muscle cell

C nerve cell

D epithelium cell

5 When DNA from two sources is combined into one single piece of DNA, it is known as

A a DNA library

B recombinant DNA

C cloned DNA

D a vector

Short answer

6 **Compare** somatic cell nuclear transfer (SCNT) with sexual fertilisation.

____

____

____

____

7 a **Compare** plasmids with bacterial chromosomes.

____

____

b **Explain** why plasmids are suitable for use in recombination experiments.

8 **Explain** why it would be especially vital to use a positive control for a PCR analysis.

9 **a** **Define** the purpose of the BLAST online database.

b **Describe** how BLAST could be used to generate phylogenetic trees.

10 **Construct** a flowchart of the Sanger method of DNA sequencing.

CHAPTER 13

The concept of evolution

This chapter begins by exploring the multiple ideas put forward to account for the origin of living organisms and their great diversity. The ideas of Aristotle, Linnaeus and Lamarck were presented as possible scientific explanations before Charles Darwin published *On the Origin of Species*. Neo-Darwinism incorporates the concept of change in the genetic composition of a population during successive generations, bringing in the genetic technologies developed in recent times. Microevolution and macroevolution are introduced, to be covered in more depth in subsequent chapters.

Fossils are the preserved remains of organisms from long ago. The age of fossils can be determined from the age of the fossil and/or the rock surrounding it. Radioactive isotopes enable scientists to calculate the age of rocks and fossils, allowing them to build a geological and evolutionary timescale of life on Earth.

Life on Earth has undergone several mass extinctions due to global environmental catastrophes, and whether the Earth is currently in its sixth mass extinction, caused largely by the actions of humans, is discussed.

Evolutionary radiation is introduced as a process by which organisms evolve to occupy new niches in their ecosystem. Darwin's finches are given as an example of adaptive radiation. Finally, the idea of the 'molecular clock', relating to the mutation rate of a particular gene, is discussed.

CHAPTER CHECKLIST

Read this checklist before you complete this chapter's activities and then return to it to check your understanding before your assessments.

Once you have completed this chapter, you can use the 'I can …' statements to assess your understanding of the topics covered by ticking the appropriate box in the 'rating column'.

I can …	Confidently	Partially	Not really
… describe how the theory of evolution came about			
… explain how fossils have helped us understand the history of Earth			
… define the different mass extinction events			
… describe evolutionary radiation			
… construct and understand a phylogenetic tree			

RESEARCH REVIEW 13

Transition fossils as evidence for evolution

Fossilised remains of organisms that have since become extinct have become one of the key pieces of evidence that supports the theory of evolution.

The following claim was suggested about fossils.

> **The fossil record often shows examples of transition fossils, those intermediate fossils that exhibit characteristics between an ancestral group and a descendant group. *Archaeopteryx*, for instance, shows a close relationship with both dinosaurs and birds.**

FIGURE 1 *Archaeopteryx* fossil, showing feather imprints

1 **Construct** a research question relating to the evidence that transition fossils support evolution.

2 Using the research question you developed about fossil evidence, use a search engine to find one credible resource and one non-credible resource. **Summarise** why they are or are not credible below.

Resource 1

Source:

Why was it credible or non-credible?

Resource 2

Source:

Why was it credible or non-credible?

Study tip

There are two types of fossils – physical remains of organisms and imprints of organisms.

EXAM EXCELLENCE 13

Multiple choice – circle the correct answer

1 Which theory, now proved incorrect, explained the formation of the different species of organisms as spontaneously formed from non-living material?

A biogenesis

B natural selection

C spontaneous generation

D neo-Darwinism

2 In the principle of rock succession:

A trilobite fossils would be found above *Dimetrodon* fossils.

B *Archaeopteryx* fossils would be found beneath *Brontosaurus* fossils.

C *Gingko* fossils would be found above *Meganeura* fossils.

D *Pterodactylus* fossils would be found above sabre-toothed tiger fossils.

3 A scientist is studying the evolution of a particular species of dinosaur. Which isotope should be measured to determine the age of the fossil specimens?

A thorium 232

B carbon 14

C uranium 235

D potassium 45

4 Identify the likely cause of the last five mass extinctions.

A rapid climate change

B flooding events

C asteroid impact

D overabundance of predators

5 An ecologist visiting the Galapagos Islands views a tree finch species that eats insects and has a probing bill. Identify the species of finch.

A warbler finch

B woodpecker finch

C sharp-beaked ground finch

D small vegetarian tree finch

Short answer

6 **List** four pieces of evidence that support the theory of evolution.

7 a **Construct** a flowchart of fossil formation.

b **Explain** why it would be unlikely to find fossils of fur or skin.

8 **Consider** the definition of a molecular clock in relation to conserved genes.

9 a **Compare** mass extinction with evolutionary radiation.

b **Deduce** why the rapid rise of mammals following the extinction of the dinosaurs occurred.

10 **Construct** a phylogenetic tree from the following DNA sequences.

Species 1: AGATCAGATCAGATCCAGTTTACAGTCATCGATC
Species 2: AGATCAGATCAGATCCAGTTTACAGTCATCGATC
Species 3: AGATCAGACCAGATCCAGTTTACAGTCATCGATC
Species 4: AGATCAGACCAGAGCCAGTTTACAGTCATCGATC
Species 5: AGATCAGACCAGAGCCAGTTTACAGTCATCGATC

CHAPTER 14

Microevolution

This chapter discusses natural selection, and how it occurs when the pressures of the environment confer a selective advantage on a specific phenotype to enhance its survivability and reproduction rate. Two basic concepts are used to introduce the modern theory of evolution: mutations cause variability in the phenotype of a population, and natural selection acts on the phenotypic variability of the population. Those organisms that produce a large number of offspring are said to have high fecundity, and there is a higher frequency of their alleles in the population's gene pool. The change to a gene pool over a succession of generations is termed 'microevolution'.

A gene pool is the sum of all the alleles of all the genes of all the individuals in a population. The alleles present may be neutral (having no effect on the survival of individuals), harmful or advantageous (to the survival of individuals).

Changing environmental conditions can affect the selection pressures for particular alleles. Distribution curves are used to demonstrate the range of alleles, and which phenotypes are most successful in the current environmental conditions. If the conditions change because of an ecosystem becoming drier, for example, the distribution curve may shift in favour of those organisms more adapted to surviving drought.

Allelic frequencies in a population can be calculated, and this calculation is given with examples. Genetic equilibrium is said to occur when the frequency of an allele in a gene pool does not change from generation to generation. Genetic drift, the founder effect and a population bottleneck may upset the genetic equilibrium of a population.

CHAPTER CHECKLIST

Read this checklist before you complete this chapter's activities and then return to it to check your understanding before your assessments.

Once you have completed this chapter, you can use the 'I can …' statements to assess your understanding of the topics covered by ticking the appropriate box in the 'rating column'.

I can …	Confidently	Partially	Not really
… describe how microevolution occurs through natural selection			
… explain how a population can vary			
… calculate gene frequencies in a population			

RESEARCH REVIEW 14

Referencing conventions

Referencing in scientific literature lends credibility to a study. It shows that there has been extensive research of the topic prior to asking the research question and developing the method.

When you are directly quoting a resource within a report, use the first author's name and year in brackets, for example: (Watson, 2019). If there is more than one author, you can use the Latin abbreviation 'et al.', meaning 'and others': (Watson et al., 2019).

At the end of the report a list of all resources should be included. Include:

- the authors (first names can be abbreviated)
- the title of the resource
- where it was printed (journal title) and which edition
- the year it was printed.

These should be in order of how they were referenced in the report.

1 On 12 February 2009, David N. Reznick and Robert E. Rocklefs wrote an article called 'Darwin's bridge between microevolution and macroevolution'. This was printed in *Nature*, an international science journal, volume 457, pages 837–42.

  a **Determine** how you would cite this resource within a report.

  b **Determine** how you would cite this resource at the end of a report.

2 According to Google Scholar, Charles Darwin's ground-breaking study *On the Origin of Species* has been cited in other studies over 42 000 times. Search online to **determine** how you would reference this study.

FIGURE 1 Charles Darwin wrote *On the Origin of Species*.

Study tip

Many word-processing programs allow assisted referencing tools, so explore their use in writing a scientific report. Each scientific journal has a slightly different style of referencing, so ask your teacher which style you are expected to use.

EXAM EXCELLENCE 14

Multiple choice – circle the correct answer

1 Define 'gene pool'.

A the total sum of all the alleles of all the individuals in the population

B the total sum of all the phenotypes in the species, regardless of geography

C the total sum of all the alleles of all the organisms in an ecosystem

D the total sum of all the genes in the genome of a population

2 A giraffe's neck, a sword-billed hummingbird's long beak, and pyrethroid resistance in head lice are all examples of:

A directional selection

B artificial selection

C disruptive selection

D genetic equilibrium

FIGURE 2 The evolution of the giraffe's neck

3 Identify the four conditions of genetic equilibrium.

A large enough population, mutational equilibrium, large immigration or emigration numbers, random reproduction

B large enough population, mutational equilibrium, no immigration or emigration, non-random reproduction

C small enough population, mutational equilibrium, no immigration or emigration, non-random reproduction

D large enough population, mutational equilibrium, no immigration or emigration, random reproduction

4 An ecologist measures the flower height of a species of banksia, finding each florescence to be on average 10 cm high. What is flower size likely to be after 10 generations of stabilising selection? What might it be after 10 generations of directional selection?

A 10 cm; 10 cm

B greater or less than 10 cm; 10 cm

C 10 cm; greater or less than 10 cm

D 10 cm; 15 cm

5 What does the term q^2 refer to in the Hardy–Weinberg equation?

A homozygous dominant

B homozygous recessive

C heterozygous

D codominant

Short answer

6 A species of wild goat develops the ability to extract nutrients from tussock grass more efficiently (phenotype B). **Identify** an event that would lead to an increase in the phenotype B goats.

____

____

7 **Select** the correct terms by circling them.

If the population is (small/large), the individual's sample of the gene pool is (small/large). However if the population is (small/large), the sample is relatively (small/large).

8 Cichlids in Lake Malawi in Africa can grow to lengths of up to 90 cm in the wild. Fish release growth-inhibiting hormones into the water around them, and nitrogen from their waste also contributes to inhibiting their growth. Fish kept in an aquarium do not reach the length of fish in Lake Malawi, although they do reach maturity and reproduce at the same age as their wild cousins. **Explain** how this may be an advantage.

9 You breed racing pigeons for the Queensland Racing Pigeon Federation. There are two pigeon colours in your pigeon loft: grey and white. You breed a grey male with a white female. They produce three chicks, a grey male and two grey females. You breed one of the female chicks with a white male. They produce three chicks from this mating: one male and one female that are grey, and one female that is white.

Use Hardy and Weinberg's equation to **calculate** the allelic frequencies, then **calculate** the expected homozygous dominant, heterozygous and homozygous recessive phenotype frequencies.

10 It has been estimated that 99% of the species that have ever lived have died out. **Discuss** the concept of natural selection in terms of species extinctions.

Speciation and macroevolution

This chapter compares different forms of evolution: divergent, parallel and convergent. Divergent evolution occurs when a population of interbreeding organisms separates into two or more descendent species. Parallel evolution occurs when two species evolve to suit similar environmental pressures but are reproductively isolated. Convergent evolution occurs when very different organisms develop similar features, such as the wings of birds and insects. Coevolution occurs when separate species exert a selective force on one another, such as two species in a predator–prey relationship.

Speciation is the development of a new species. This can occur when the gene pool of one population differs significantly from the gene pool of other populations, so the populations can no longer interbreed to produce viable offspring. The geography of the environment can contribute to this. For example, a population living at different heights on a mountain can vary over its range (clinal variation). A geographical barrier can cause populations to become isolated from one another. When two populations of an organism are isolated from each other, evolve into separate species, and later reconnect, the phenotypes of the two populations may be blended together, giving rise to zones of hybridisation. Reproductive isolation – including seasonal, behavioural and geographical – can lead to speciation.

The types of speciation, including allopatric (when the populations have separate ranges), parapatric (the populations have slightly overlapping ranges) and sympatric (the species coexist in the same range), are explained. Scientists are able to analyse gene flow data and have identified examples of these. Macroevolution, referring to major evolutionary change over time, is defined, and examples of key patterns of evolution, including stasis, character changes, and lineage splitting, are provided. Extinction, when the biotic and abiotic conditions cause the demise of an entire species, is discussed. Finally, the evolution of humans is described using fossil records and DNA analysis.

CHAPTER CHECKLIST

Read this checklist before you complete this chapter's activities and then return to it to check your understanding before your assessments.

Once you have completed this chapter, you can use the 'I can …' statements to assess your understanding of the topics covered by ticking the appropriate box in the 'rating column'.

I can …	Confidently	Partially	Not really
… describe how a species can diversify			
… define speciation and how it occurs			
… explain the different modes of speciation			
… explain reproductive isolation			
… describe macroevolution			

RESEARCH REVIEW 15

Conclusions, correlations and causations

There are many datasets that correlate but aren't causally related. For instance, as the sale of ice-cream increases, so does the sale of sunglasses. However, these are not directly related, meaning changing one variable does not cause a change in the other. Sunscreen sales increasing with temperature is an example of a causal correlation, in which the ambient temperature leads to an increase in sunscreen sales as more people purchase and use sunscreen before heading outside. However, the correlation between increased sales of ice-cream and sunglasses is not causal.

FIGURE 1 Sunglasses and ice-cream sales are not causally related.

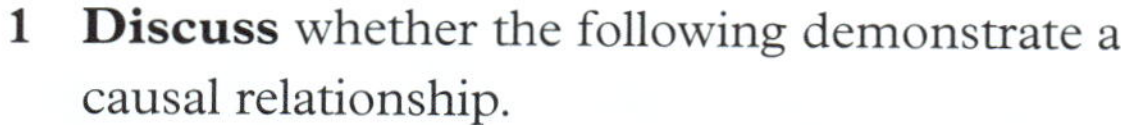

1 **Discuss** whether the following demonstrate a causal relationship.

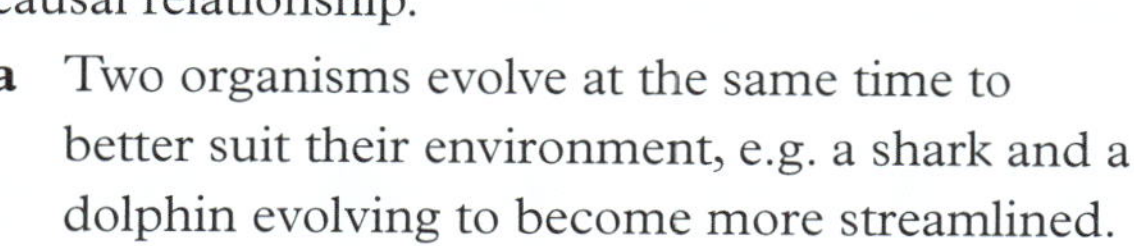

   a Two organisms evolve at the same time to better suit their environment, e.g. a shark and a dolphin evolving to become more streamlined.

   b A predator and prey species evolve new strategies for survival, e.g. cheetahs and antelopes becoming increasingly agile and faster.

   c A species evolves to better suit its environment, e.g. plants evolving in response to a reduction in rainfall.

Study tip

When reviewing a conclusion in a study, make sure to consider any causal relationship claimed by the author closely. Could there be another plausible explanation for the correlation?

EXAM EXCELLENCE 15

Multiple choice – circle the correct answer

1 Darwin's finches are an example of:

A convergent evolution

B divergent evolution

C coevolution

D parallel evolution

2 Define allopatric speciation.

A speciation due to geography

B speciation due to a broad distribution range

C speciation due to polyploidy within the same range

D development of a new individual from an unfertilised egg

3 In the past 100 000 years, humans migrated to nearly every continent on Earth. The different traits, such as skin colour, were therefore selected to help them survive in a multitude of environments. However, humans are still one species and can interbreed, giving birth to fertile offspring. What is this an example of?

A zonal hybridisation

B geographic isolates

C clinal variation

D speciation

4 The development of feathers in many dinosaurs was for insulation but acted as a mechanism that allowed early birds to fly. What is this an example of?

A extinction

B lineage splitting

C stasis

D exaptation

5 Which of the following would not cause an evolutionary bottleneck?

A bushfires

B habitat destruction

C two populations mingling

D over-predation

Short answer

6 The mimic octopus (*Thaumoctopus mimicus*) is capable of mimicking the shape and behaviour of other marine animals, including fish and crabs. It can even change colours and patterns on its skin. **Consider** why it is important that an animal mimics behaviour as well as physical appearance, as a survival strategy.

7 The development of a new species can take place in two general ways:

i through microevolution of a species into a new species, as seen in horse evolution

ii through the splitting of a species into two or more groups that evolve independently of one another, such as the giant lobelia of East Africa.

Identify an example of two species, not listed, that have developed through each of these ways.

8 **a** Bears from the *Ursus* genus have been known to hybridise in some instances. In 1876, in Germany, a mating between a brown bear and a polar bear in a zoo produced fertile offspring. **Determine**, using the diagram below, what stage the two species are currently at.

b Polar bears in the Arctic Circle and brown bears in northern Canada and Russia are closely related, but until recently their habitats did not overlap. **Suggest** a reason their habitats now overlap, allowing for hybrids in the wild and the development of a new species.

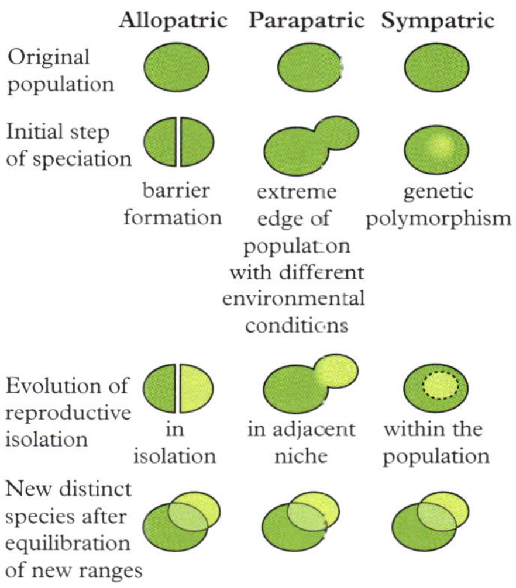

FIGURE 2 Different stages of evolution

9 Many plants adapted to sand plains and winter rain in southern Western Australia will not thrive in eastern Queensland with humid, wet summers. **Explain** what type of isolation this is an example of.

10 Many genealogy organisations offer DNA analysis to determine the ancestral history of a client's genome. A set of results is shown below:

- 68% Scandinavian
- 24% Central European
- 5% British Isles
- 3% Neanderthal.

Explain to the client where the Neanderthal DNA could have come from.

UNIT 4

PRACTICE ASSESSMENT

Heredity and continuity of life

Throughout the chapters in this unit, you have practised conducting research.

In this section, you will complete the following internal assessment:

- the Research investigation (20%).

Note: These assessments may not reflect the QCAA assessments. However, they build on the skills required for each internal assessment.

Unit 4 Research investigation

CASE STUDY

Mass extinctions

Most people can confidently list one major mass extinction event, and most likely it will be the end of the dinosaur era, the K-T boundary. However, the mass extinction event that occurred at the end of the Cretaceous period was the fifth such event to occur since life on Earth began.

In the Ordovician–Silurian extinction event, 450–440 million years ago, 86% of life on Earth became extinct. This has been attributed to glaciation and falling sea levels. The majority of life was found in the oceans at this time.

The Late Devonian extinction event, where 70% of all species became extinct, occurred 375–360 million years ago. The cause of this extinction is unclear; some theories include underwater volcanic activity, global cooling or a meteorite. This extinction event is estimated to have lasted for a few million years.

At the end of the Permian era, 252 million years ago, the Permian–Triassic extinction event occurred, which caused the extinction of up to 96% of all species. Vast populations of marine life, insects and plants became extinct. This event was most likely a result of severe climate change and has been called 'The Great Dying'.

The fourth mass extinction event, occurring 201 million years ago at the end of the Triassic period, saw 75% of all species become extinct. From this event the dinosaurs arose from *archosauria* to occupy vacant niches left by other species.

The fifth mass extinction event is probably the most well-known, marking the end of the Cretaceous period and the age of the dinosaurs. Attributed to a major meteorite in the Yucatan Peninsula near modern-day Mexico, there has since been evidence that there was a decline in the population of species prior to the meteorite, most likely due to changes in climate and volcanic activity. At this time 75% of all species became extinct.

FIGURE 1 A large number of species are at risk of becoming extinct on Earth; the polar bear is one of them.

Your task is to conduct a Research investigation about the following claim, which is related to the case study above:

We are currently in the sixth mass extinction event, this one being caused by one species: humans.

Research question

Research

Resource 1

- Title:
- Authors:
- Source and credibility:
- Publication date:
- Aim:
- Resource's research question:
- Methodology
  - What data were collected?
  - How were the data collected?
- Results
  - Did the resource support your research question?
  - Why does/doesn't it support the provided claim?

Resource 2

- Title:
- Authors:
- Source and credibility:
- Publication date:
- Aim:
- Resource's research question:
- Methodology
  - What data were collected?
  - How were the data collected?
- Results
  - Did the resource support your research question?
  - Why does/doesn't it support the provided claim?

Planning your internal assessment

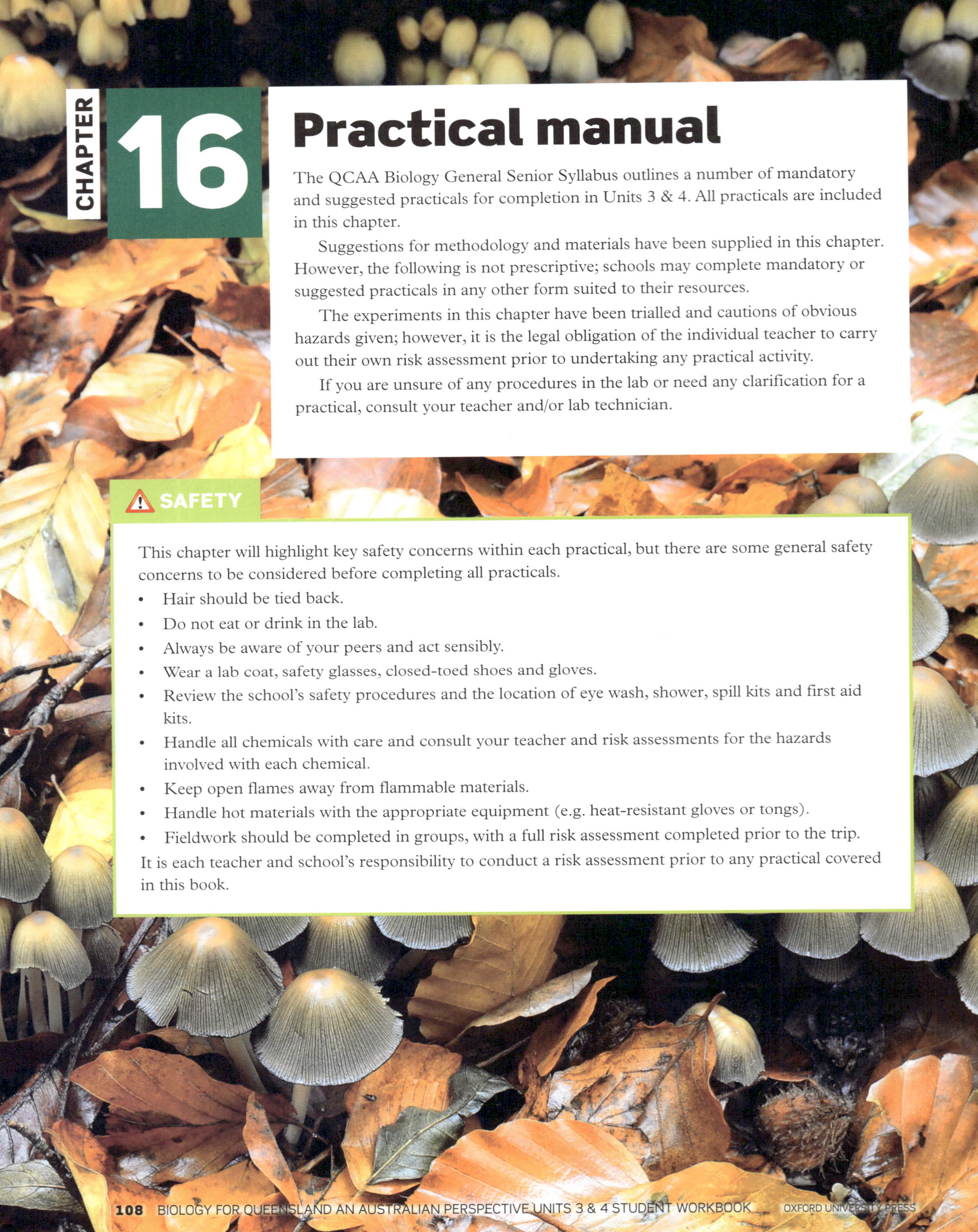

CHAPTER 16

Practical manual

The QCAA Biology General Senior Syllabus outlines a number of mandatory and suggested practicals for completion in Units 3 & 4. All practicals are included in this chapter.

Suggestions for methodology and materials have been supplied in this chapter. However, the following is not prescriptive; schools may complete mandatory or suggested practicals in any other form suited to their resources.

The experiments in this chapter have been trialled and cautions of obvious hazards given; however, it is the legal obligation of the individual teacher to carry out their own risk assessment prior to undertaking any practical activity.

If you are unsure of any procedures in the lab or need any clarification for a practical, consult your teacher and/or lab technician.

SAFETY

This chapter will highlight key safety concerns within each practical, but there are some general safety concerns to be considered before completing all practicals.

- Hair should be tied back.
- Do not eat or drink in the lab.
- Always be aware of your peers and act sensibly.
- Wear a lab coat, safety glasses, closed-toed shoes and gloves.
- Review the school's safety procedures and the location of eye wash, shower, spill kits and first aid kits.
- Handle all chemicals with care and consult your teacher and risk assessments for the hazards involved with each chemical.
- Keep open flames away from flammable materials.
- Handle hot materials with the appropriate equipment (e.g. heat-resistant gloves or tongs).
- Fieldwork should be completed in groups, with a full risk assessment completed prior to the trip.

It is each teacher and school's responsibility to conduct a risk assessment prior to any practical covered in this book.

Analysing vegetation patterns using a transect line

Part A – Measure abiotic factors in the classroom using field samples (e.g. pH, nitrogen nutrients, salinity, carbonates, turbidity) – Suggested practical

Part B – Measure abiotic factors in the field (e.g. dissolved oxygen, light, temperature, wind speed, infiltration rate) – Suggested practical

Part A and B – Use appropriate technology, such as data loggers, chemical tests, turbidity tubes and other equipment to measure factors – Manipulative skill

Part C – Determine species diversity of a group of organisms based on a given index – Mandatory practical

Aims

1 To use data collected from a transect profile to:

- **a** measure a variety of abiotic factors along a transect
- **b** determine the relative abundance of a species and families of plants
- **c** calculate and compare densities of plant species and families across an ecosystem
- **d** calculate and compare species diversity across an ecosystem
- **e** determine possible relationships between chosen plant species and abiotic conditions

Materials

Class requirement:

- 100 metre length of rope marked at 5 metre intervals (transect line)

For each group in the field:

- Laboratory thermometer
- Wet-and-dry bulb thermometer
- Light meter (LUX)
- Anemometer
- Compass
- Ribbon or cloth on a stick (wind direction)
- Trowel
- Sample bottles for soil (4)
- 500 mL deionised/distilled water
- Spirit level
- Metre ruler and plastic 30 cm ruler
- Ziploc plastic bags with labels
- Pencil and marker pen
- Clipboard
- Paper to record data

For each group in the laboratory:

- Plant family identification key
- Universal indicator
- Talcum powder
- Evaporating dish or watch glass (small)
- Digital scales
- Drying oven (set to 100°C)
- Measuring cylinder
- Beaker
- Stopwatch
- Soil testing kit (measures pH, salinity, nitrogen content, turbidity, carbonates, etc.)
- Petri dish
- Cross-wire projection tube
- 10 metres of builder's string (brightly coloured)
- Solid isosceles triangle

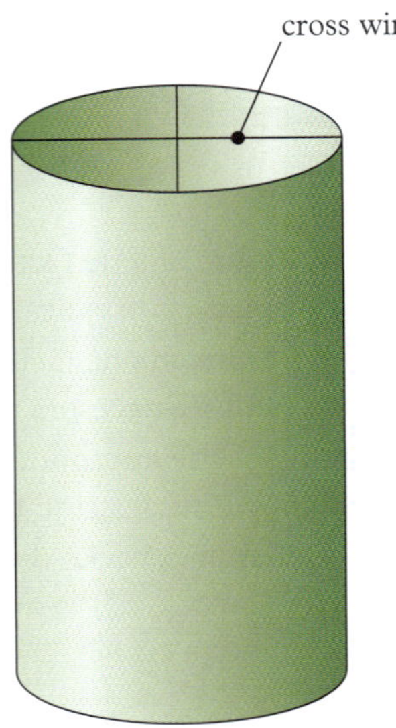

FIGURE 1 The cross-wire projection tube apparatus

Method

Part A

Measure abiotic factors in the field – Suggested practical

1 Temperature
   - Collect monthly average maximum and minimum daily temperatures from the Bureau of Meteorology (BOM) website for the area under investigation.
   - Dig a narrow hole 10 cm deep. Place the thermometer in the hole and gently refill the hole. After 3 minutes, remove the thermometer and record the temperature.
   - Measure and record the temperature at the soil surface.
   - Measure and record the temperature 1 m above the soil.

2 Relative humidity

TABLE 1 Wet bulb globe temperature (WBGT) from temperature and relative humidity

TEMPERATURE (°C)

RELATIVE HUMIDITY (%)	20	21	22	23	24	25	26	27	28	29	30	31	32	33	34	35	36	37	38	39	40	41	42	43	44	45	46	47	48	49	50
0	15	16	16	17	18	18	19	19	20	20	21	22	22	23	23	24	24	25	25	26	27	27	28	28	29	29	30	31	31	32	32
5	16	16	17	18	18	19	19	20	21	21	22	22	23	24	24	25	26	26	27	27	28	29	29	30	31	31	32	33	33	34	35
10	16	17	17	18	19	19	20	21	21	22	23	23	24	25	25	26	27	27	28	29	30	30	31	32	32	33	34	35	36	36	37
15	17	17	18	19	19	20	21	21	22	23	23	24	25	26	26	27	28	29	29	30	31	32	33	33	34	35	36	37	38	39	
20	17	18	18	19	20	21	21	22	23	24	24	25	26	27	27	28	29	30	31	32	32	33	34	35	36	37	38	39			
25	18	18	19	20	20	21	22	23	24	24	25	26	27	28	28	29	30	31	32	33	34	35	36	37	38	39					
30	18	19	20	20	21	22	23	23	24	25	26	27	28	29	29	30	31	32	33	34	35	36	37	39							
35	18	19	20	21	22	22	23	24	25	26	27	28	29	30	31	32	33	34	35	36	37	38	39								
40	19	20	21	21	22	23	24	25	26	27	28	29	30	31	32	33	34	35	36	37	38	39									
45	19	20	21	22	23	24	25	26	27	27	28	29	30	32	33	34	35	36	37	38											
50	20	21	22	23	23	24	25	26	27	28	29	30	31	33	34	35	36	37	39												
55	20	21	22	23	24	25	26	27	28	29	30	31	32	34	35	36	37	38													
60	21	22	23	24	25	26	27	28	29	30	31	32	33	35	36	37	38														
65	21	22	23	24	25	26	27	28	29	31	32	33	34	36	37	38															
70	22	23	24	25	26	27	28	29	30	31	33	34	35	36	38	39										WBGT > 40					
75	22	23	24	25	26	27	29	30	31	32	33	35	36	37	39																
80	23	24	25	26	27	28	29	30	32	33	34	36	37	38																	
85	23	24	25	26	28	29	30	31	32	34	35	37	38	39																	
90	24	25	26	27	28	29	31	32	33	35	36	37	39																		
95	24	25	26	27	29	30	31	33	34	35	37	38																			
100	24	26	27	28	29	31	32	33	35	36	38	39																			

Note: This table is compiled from an approximate formula that only depends on temperature and humidity. The formula is valid for full sunshine and a light wind.

- Use the wet-bulb and dry-bulb thermometers and the conversion chart to measure the relative humidity at both soil level and 1 m above the ground. Record the results.

3 Light intensity

- Use the light meter to measure and record the light intensity at ground level.

4 Wind

- Use the anemometer to measure and record the wind speed at both ground level and 1 m above the ground.

  1 knot = 1.853 km/h
  = 0.514 m/s

- Determine the direction of the wind using a cloth tied on a stick and, using the compass, record the bearings.

5 Soil testing in the field

- Humus
  - Using the trowel, dig a hole in the soil. Use the ruler to measure the depth of the topsoil (dark-coloured). Record this measurement. Measure and record the depth of leaf litter and humus (decayed plant and animal organic matter) on top of the soil.
- Texture
  - Place a handful of soil in your hand and moisten with water. Roll the wet soil and record features such as the ability to form a ball (indicating a high clay content), or grittiness. Use the diagram below to determine the type of soil. Record your data.

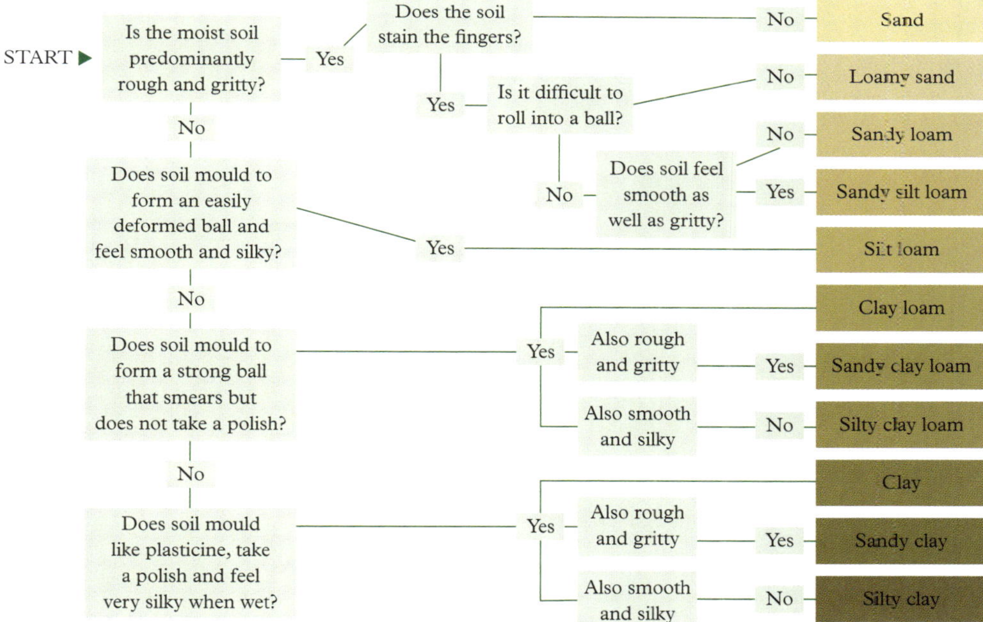

FIGURE 2 A flowchart to determine the type of soil present

  - Collect samples of soil in the sample bottles and sealable plastic bag to take back to the laboratory for testing: if the selected transect is sloped, soil samples should be collected from the top and bottom sections of the transect.

6 Rainfall

- Complete a computer search and record the average yearly rainfall for the area as well as the average for the month at the time of observation from the BOM website.
- Record all the results from 1 to 6 in a table and any other observations.

Observations

TABLE 2 Abiotic measurements in the field

Site location	
Group members	
Date	
Factors	**Measurement**
Temperature soil surface	
Temperature 1 m above soil	
Relative humidity	
Light intensity at ground level	
Wind direction	
Depth of topsoil	
Depth of leaf litter and humus	
Type of soil	
Average yearly rainfall	
Average monthly rainfall	

7 Physiography

- Run a 100 m transect line through a *typical* part of the habitat.
- Use the compass to record the direction of the transect, and in dense vegetation ensure you maintain the compass bearing.
- Using the equipment provided, measure the slope as described below. You will need four students: A, B, C and D.

a A goes to the highest point of the area to be profiled and holds one end of the string on the ground. B and C walk downhill with the other end of the string until they are 1 m below A, or 10 m away from A, whichever comes first.

b In either case, the string is held against B, at a height that keeps the string level.

c C then walks back to the middle of the interval and uses the line spirit level to check that the string is level, and B makes adjustments up or down as is necessary.

d C then walks along the line, measuring and calling out the distance that C is along the string from A and the height of the string at that point, so that these can be recorded by D. Heights are recorded as often as is needed for an accurate profile.

e A then moves down to where B is, and B and C start all over again, remembering to add on the drop-in height from where A was to where B was.

f Reverse the system when you are going uphill.

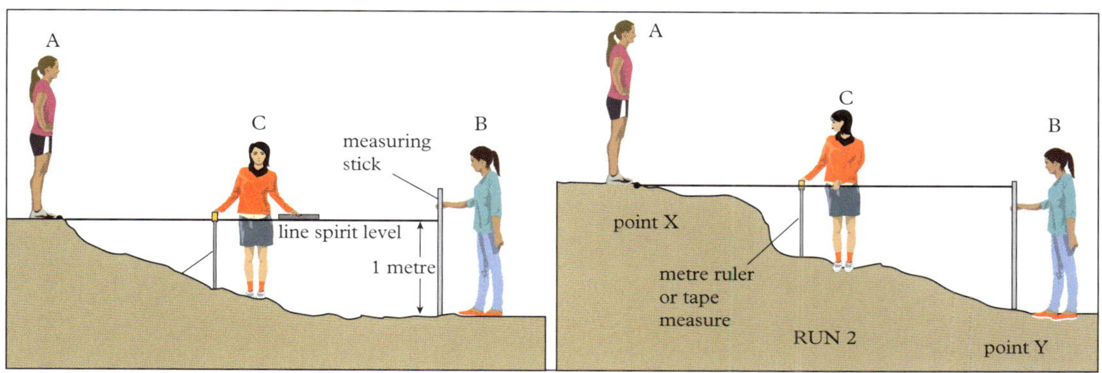

Measuring a land surface profile: from the starting point

Measuring a land surface profile: continuing further down the slope

FIGURE 3 Two diagrams showing how to measure land surface profiles

Record your results in the table below with distance from the start and depth (in metres).

TABLE 3 Transect in the field

Transect direction	
Distance from start (A)	**Depth (m)**

Method

Part B

Measuring abiotic factors in the laboratory – Suggested practical

Soil testing in the laboratory:

- pH
  - Place a small amount of the collected soil in a Petri dish. Sprinkle a fine layer of talcum powder over the soil. Add a few drops of universal indicator and observe the colour. Using the colour chart, determine and record the soil pH.
- Moisture
  - Zero an electronic balance and weigh the evaporating dish/watch glass to at least 2 decimal places. Record weight. Place approximately 10 g (using a large spatula) of soil from the sealed plastic bag onto the evaporating dish/watch glass, spread evenly across the bottom of the dish and reweigh. Record weight. (weight a) Place the dish in an oven at 100°C for 24 hours. Using heat-proof gloves remove from the oven and place in a desiccator to cool to room temperature. Reweigh dish and soil. (weight b) The difference between the two weights (weight a – weight b) provides a measure of water content. Record as grams of water per 10 grams of soil.

    ____

    ____

    ____

- Soil air content
  - Place a sample of soil in beaker and weigh the contents (weight of 'soil'). Slowly add water until the water is level with the top of the soil. Reweigh the beaker and its contents (weight of 'soil + water'). Determine the amount of water in the soil from ('soil + water' – 'soil'). As 1 g water is equivalent to 1 cm^3 and the amount of water measures the amount of air displaced, determine the soil air content in the sample.

    ____

    ____

    ____

- Soil mineral content
  - Using the soil mineral test kit, follow the provided instructions and record the levels of the minerals present.

TABLE 4 Abiotic measurements in the laboratory

Soil factors	Measurement
pH	
Moisture content	
Soil air content	
Mineral content	

Method

Part C

Determine species diversity – Mandatory practical

1 Run a transect line 100 m through the same section of vegetation used for the land profile. Consider the transect line as a strip 10 cm wide along each side of the string. Different groups of students can run adjoining parallel transect lines approximately 5 m apart. Take care not to trample plants along each transect line.

2 At the first 5 m interval, examine the plants directly beneath, touching or overhanging the string at the interval mark. Identify the plant(s) to family level using the key provided by your teacher. Take a sample of leaves, flowers and fruit (where present) and place in the plastic bag. Label each specimen as species A, B, etc. Record on the bag label any details (herb, shrub, tree, etc.) and any distinguishing features such as height, and colour of the bark. The specimens will be the reference set for the same species at different sites along the transect line and can be used for later identification of species (e.g. from plant guides, or dried plants and photos can be sent to a herbarium). Record the plants on your data sheet. For recording it is best to study each stratum (ground, shrubs, trees) separately.

3 Repeat step 2 at every 5 m interval along the transect line. This will give a total of 20 stations for each transect line. Add new species bags to your specimen collection as you encounter them.

4 At each 5 m interval, determine and record the foliage cover using the crosswire tube, at both ground level and the canopy. Take note of the tallest plant and percentage of foliage cover.

Results

TABLE 5 Plant identification along transect

Distance from start of transect	Notes	Plant names (family level)	Plant names (species level)

Distance from start of transect	Notes	Plant names (family level)	Plant names (species level)

Analysing the data

1 In the laboratory, identify the species from plant guides (enter species names in Table 5). A collection of plants that cannot be identified in this way can be sent to a herbarium for identification. If plants cannot be identified, give them a code name, e.g. Species A, Species B, etc. Identified species can be logged at the Atlas of Living Australia (https://biocache.ala.org.au/explore/your-area).

2 Count the total number of families and total number of different species encountered.

3 Use this information to calculate Simpson's Diversity Index:

- Simpson's Diversity Index (*SDI*):

$$SDI = 1 - \frac{\Sigma n(n-1)}{N(N-1)}$$

where n is the total number of individuals of a particular species; N is the total number of all individuals counted (from all species); $\Sigma n(n-1)$ means to calculate $n(n-1)$ for each species surveyed, then add them all together. The closer the *SDI* value is to 1, the more diverse the community; i.e. one species is not more prevalent than the others.

4 Repeat step 3 for the families. Enter the results for '3' and '4' in Table 6.

TABLE 6 Species and family diversity

Species Simpson's Diversity Index	Family Simpson's Diversity Index

5 Calculate the percentage foliage cover for both the ground cover and canopy layers cover:

$$\% \text{ foliage cover} = \frac{\text{number of foliage sites recorded}}{\text{number of observation sites}} \times 100$$

6 Classify the ecosystem using this calculation and Specht's structural classification of vegetation (Table 7).

TABLE 7 Specht's structural classification of Australian vegetation

Growth form of tallest stratum	Foliage cover by the tallest stratum			
	>70%	30–70%	10–30%	<10%
Tall trees (>30 m)	Tall closed forest	Tall open forest	Tall woodland	
Medium trees (10–30 m)	Closed forest	Open forest	Woodland	Open woodland
Low trees (<10 m)	Low closed forest	Low open forest	Low woodland	Low open woodland
Tall shrubs (>2 m)	Closed scrub	Open scrub	Tall scrubland	Tall open scrubland
Low shrubs (<2 m)	Closed heath	Open heath	Low shrubland	Low open shrubland
Hummock grasses			Hummock grassland	
Tufted/tussock grasses	Closed tussock grassland	Tussock grassland	Open tussock grassland	Dense open grassland
Graminoids	Closed sedgeland	Sedgeland	Open sedgeland	
Other herbaceous species	Dense sown pasture	Sown pasture	Open herb field	Sparse open herb field

Sketching a transect is not required for this practical, but is a handy skill used by biologists. If you have access, directions for this can be found in the *Biology for Queensland An Australian Perspective Units 3 & 4* Student obook assess.

Discussion

Write a discussion of your results including the following points:

- the level of species diversity in the two transects and possible reasons for this
- explanation of why density was not calculated and a possible means of determining density given the sampling method
- relationship between the vegetation observed and abiotic factors.

Note: There is more space to write out your discussion points in Practical 3.8B, pages 119–20.

Stratified sampling of vegetation patterns

Use the process of stratified sampling to collect and analyse primary biotic and abiotic field data to classify an ecosystem.

Source: *Biology 2019 v1.2 General Senior Syllabus* © Queensland Curriculum & Assessment Authority

This investigation could be carried out in conjunction with Practical 3.8A as part of a full day field trip. Identify two related areas of a local ecosystem to compare the vegetation patterns. Alternatively, if time is an issue, students can combine results from other group's transects, or different aspects of the same transect, in order to compare between two transects.

Aims

1 To use data collected from two different transect profiles within a habitat to:

- **a** measure abiotic factors in the transects
- **b** determine the relative abundance of a species and families of plants
- **c** calculate relative densities of species and families
- **d** examine the family groups of plants present within a particular community to determine whether there is a relationship between particular types of plants
- **e** compare the data from the two transects and determine similarities and differences in abiotic and biotic components

Materials

See methods for Practical 3.8A.

Method

See methods for Practical 3.8A.

Observations

____

____

____

____

Results

TABLE 1 Abiotic measurements

Site location	
Group members	
Date	
Factors	**Measurement**
Temperature of soil surface	

Temperature 1 m above soil	
Relative humidity	
Light intensity at ground level	
Wind direction	
Depth of topsoil	
Depth of leaf litter and humus	
Type of soil	
Average yearly rainfall	
Average monthly rainfall	

TABLE 2 Transect in the field

Transect direction	
Distance from start (A)	**Depth (m)**

Moisture content calculations

Soil air content calculations

TABLE 3 Abiotic measurements in the laboratory

Soil factors	Measurement
pH	
Moisture content	
Soil air content	
Mineral content	

TABLE 4 Plant identification along transect

Distance from start of transect	Notes	Plant names (family level)	Plant names (species level)

Distance from start of transect	Notes	Plant names (family level)	Plant names (species level)

Simpson's Diversity Index calculations

TABLE 5 Species and family diversity

Species Simpson's Diversity Index	Family Simpson's Diversity Index

Discussion

Write a discussion of your results including the following points:

- determination of whether certain species or families occur throughout the habitat
- possible reasons for any grouping of species
- the level of species diversity in the two transects and possible reasons for this
- relationship between the vegetation observed and abiotic factors.
- compare your results to the previous transect in practical 3.8A.

Conclusion

Write a brief summary of your findings for practicals 3.8A and 3.8B.

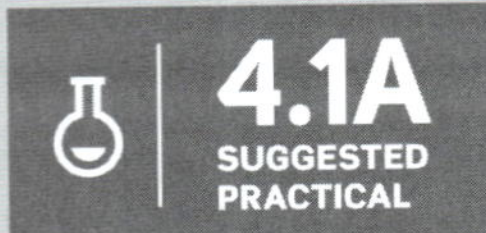

A simplified food chain in leaf litter

Study the abundance of each trophic level in a simple food chain.

Source: *Biology 2019 v1.2 General Senior Syllabus* © Queensland Curriculum & Assessment Authority

Aims

1 To collect and identify leaf litter organisms
2 To determine a simple food chain from the collected organisms
3 To determine the abundance of autotrophs, herbivores and carnivores in the selected food chain

Materials

- Four 25 × 25 cm quadrats (students can use straws and tape or sticks in the field)
- Garden gloves
- Four large Ziploc bags
- Light source
- Four Berlese–Tullgren funnels
- Four 500 mL collection jars
- Large sheet of paper
- Four Petri dishes
- Forceps and fine paintbrush
- Sheet of photographs of common animals
- Preserving alcohol or rubbing alcohol (approximately 1–2 cm in the bottom of each jar)

Method

1 Select an area of undisturbed leaf litter 10 m × 10 m.
2 Four students, with backs facing this area, are to throw the quadrats into the sampling area. This will give a total sample size of 100 cm × 100 cm.
3 With gardening gloves on (spiders and centipedes may be present in the litter), carefully place all the litter within the quadrat into a plastic bag and seal it.
4 In the laboratory set up the Berlese–Tullgren funnels and light sources on the side benches where they will not be disturbed. Half-fill each collecting jar with preserving alcohol.
5 Leave the equipment set up for 24 hours to allow extraction of all litter organisms.

FIGURE 1 A modified Berlese–Tullgren funnel set up for litter extraction: a known volume of soil or litter is placed on the sieve in the funnel. When the light above the funnel is switched on, the organisms move downwards to avoid the light, heat and drying effects of the globe. In doing so, they fall into the jar containing preservative.

6 Turn off the light and spread the leaf litter from each sample separately onto a large sheet of paper. Count and record the number of leaves present in the sample in Table 1. If any animals have died from dehydration before moving through the funnel, add these to the animal counts.
7 Decant off extra preservative from the collection beaker. Transfer the litter animals to a Petri dish.
8 Using the forceps or paintbrush, carefully separate each type of animal into groups – ants in one group, centipedes in another group, and so on. Count and record the number of each type in Table 1.
9 Identify each type of organism to genus level (http://anic.ento.csiro.au/insectfamilies/)
10 Research the food requirements of each organism (leaf eater, eats ants, eats slaters, etc.)
11 Discard any animals that do not fit into a simple food chain from the surveyed organisms (e.g. fungal eaters or bacterial eaters). Choose a maximum of five organisms.

TABLE 1 Organism counts in leaf litter

Organism	Count	Food requirements	Percent abundance (per 1 m^2)
Leaves			

Results

1 Draw the food chain.

2 Combine the scores of the selected organisms for the food chain and multiply by 1. This gives the total abundance per 1 m^2. Now divide the count of each organism by total abundance and multiply by 100 to calculate the percent abundance of each organism. Record your results in Table 1.

3 Draw a pyramid of numbers for the food web.

Discussion

Write a discussion of your results including the following points:

- Describe the limitations of the method of collecting data.
- Name any difficulties encountered in constructing a food chain.
- Describe and explain the shape of the pyramid of numbers.
- From the data collected, is this a complete food chain? Justify your response.
- Suggest any impact on the food chain if the area had been regularly sprayed for weeds.
- Suggest possible improvements for collecting data.

Conclusion

Write a brief summary of your findings.

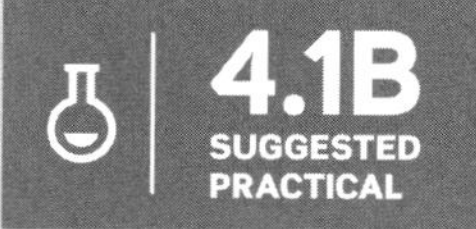

Measuring biomass

Measure the wet biomass of producer samples.

Source: *Biology 2019 v1.2 General Senior Syllabus* © Queensland Curriculum & Assessment Authority

Aim

To compare and contrast the wet and dry biomass of several samples of producers

Materials

- Five 25 × 35 cm Ziploc plastic bags
- Digital scales
- Paper
- Oven
- Desiccator containing a drying agent (e.g. blue silica gel)
- Baking paper

Method

1 Completely fill each bag with green leaves from five different types of plant, immediately sealing each bag once it is full. Label each bag with the plant name and the number of plants from which the material was collected (e.g. with short grasses it may take 20 plants to fill the bag, but only a couple for taller grasses, or one plant if it is a tree or shrub).

2 Weigh and record each sample in Table 1.

3 Compare the wet biomass (before drying) with the number of plants from which the leaves were collected. (This is a rough comparison only, since it is unlikely that all the leaves from a shrub or tree would fit into one bag.) Also compare the wet biomass of the same volume for the different types of species present.

4 Carefully measure 10 g of material from each sample and place the 10 g samples onto individual pieces of paper. Spread the material out as much as possible. Label each with the plant name.

5 Place the plant material in an oven at 105°C on baking paper for approximately 24 hours. When the leaves are completely dry but not charred, remove them from the oven and place in a desiccator to cool to room temperature. Reweigh each sample. Record the weight in Table 1.

6 Calculate the weight of the water (wet weight minus dry weight) and percentage of water (weight of water ÷ wet weight × 100) in each sample.

7 Compare the dry biomass of the different species by entering values into Table 1.

Results

TABLE 1 Samples and their biomass

Plant	Wet biomass (A) in grams	Number of plants (B)	Dried biomass (C)	Mass of water in wet biomass (A – C)	Percentage of water in sample (Mass of water / A) × 100

Discussion

Write a discussion of your results including the following points:

- Why is it important to know biomass of an organism in an area?
- Why should dry weight rather than wet weight be used to determine biomass?
- What is the relationship between biomass and productivity?
- How can this experiment be improved?
- Suggest a possible technique for determining biomass of small invertebrates (e.g. the number of ants or earthworms found in a 1 m^3 of soil).

Conclusion

Write a brief summary of your findings.

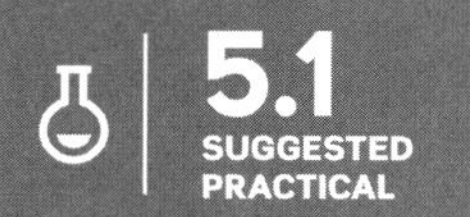

Plant distribution and abundance using quadrats

Conduct an abundance and distribution study, including abiotic and biotic factors.

Source: *Biology 2019 v1.2 General Senior Syllabus* © Queensland Curriculum & Assessment Authority

Aims

1 To estimate the percentage coverage of grass in a lawn or on an oval, football field, etc. – Part A

2 To estimate the distribution and abundance of the weeds growing in the study area – Part B

Five areas are to be selected at random. Devise a way to achieve this and include it in your results.

Materials

Class requires:

- Trundle wheel (optional) for measuring the oval or field

Each group requires:

- 1 × 1 m quadrat
- Pen or pencil for recording results

Method

A Estimation of how much of the oval is covered by grass (percentage coverage)

1 Set up the quadrat randomly on the oval.

2 Make an estimation of the percentage grass cover of the area within the quadrat. There is no need to distinguish between the different types of grass; however, record how many different types of grass that you think are present.

3 Repeat this procedure four more times and record your five results in Table 1 below.

4 Estimate the area of the study, i.e. the size of the oval.

Results

1 Average your five results.

2 Record the averaged results from the other groups in your class in the lines below and average those, and then record them in Table 1. This gives the class average percentage of grass coverage per square metre.

Group averages:

____

____

____

TABLE 1 Percentage coverage of grass on the oval

Quadrat number	Percentage grass cover (%)	Estimated number of grass types
1		
2		

Quadrat number	Percentage grass cover (%)	Estimated number of grass types
3		
4		
5		
Average (per m^2)		
Class average (per m^2)		

3 Estimate the percentage area of grass coverage for the entire oval (average/m^2 × area of oval).

Method

B Determination of the distribution and abundance of weeds growing in the study area

1 As a class determine an identification system for the weeds in the area. As it is unlikely that you will know the names of the weeds, call the first weed Weed A, and describe it using features such as leaf shape, size and colour, flower shape and colour (a quick sketch or photograph could be of assistance). Continue as each new weed is encountered.

2 Set the quadrat on the grass and lay out the identification system from step 1.
3 Count the number of weeds of each different type found in the quadrat.
4 Repeat this procedure four more times. Positioning of the quadrats must be random.

Results

1 Record your five results in Table 2 and average them for each weed species.
2 Collect the results from the other groups in your class for each weed species and average them (= class average). Record these results in Table 2.

Group results:

TABLE 2 Number of weeds in oval (per m^2)

	Quadrat number						
Weed	1	2	3	4	5	Average number of weeds	Class average number of weeds
A							
B							
C							
D							

3 Estimate the number of each species for the entire oval.

Discussion

Write a discussion of your results, including the following points.

Part A

- How closely do your average results compare with the class average? Provide explanations for any discrepancies.
- How well do the results compare with your impression of the area? Provide explanations for any discrepancies.
- How random were the placements of the quadrats? Explain your answer.
- Could there have been any bias in the placement of the quadrats, e.g. staying in the sun on a cold morning?

Part B

- Was there any domination of the area by one particular weed? Suggest possible reasons for this.
- Did the distribution and abundance of different weeds vary in different areas of the oval? Make some suggestions as to why this could occur. Design an experiment to test these suggestions.

- Was the methodology used accurate? To answer this, compare the percentage coverage with an actual count of each individual area enclosed by the quadrat.
- What are the advantages of each method for:
  - the estimation of population density (population size) of the dominant weed in the study area?
  - the accuracy of the estimation of the total population of the dominant weed?
  - the use of the quadrat method for determining the abundance of moving organisms?
- Devise a method to estimate the abundance of the different types of birds around the school.

Conclusion

Write a brief summary of your findings.

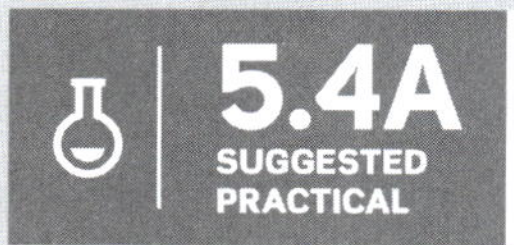

Competitive exclusion in *Paramecium*

Test the competitive exclusion principle hypothesis.

Source: *Biology 2019 v1.2 General Senior Syllabus* © Queensland Curriculum & Assessment Authority

Aims

1 To carry out an experiment to determine one of the following hypotheses:
- In a mixed culture of *Paramecium caudatum* and *Paramecium aurelia*, *Paramecium caudatum* will not survive.
- In a mixed culture of *Paramecium caudatum* and *Paramecium aurelia*, *Paramecium aurelia* will not survive.
- In a mixed culture of *Paramecium caudatum* and *Paramecium aurelia*, if one species survives, the species that survives will have the higher carrying capacity.
- In a mixed culture of *Paramecium caudatum* and *Paramecium aurelia*, both species will survive at a lower carrying capacity than when in a single colony.

2 Devise a method to count the *Paramecium* individuals in each sample.

Materials

- Microscope
- Pure cultures of *P. caudatum* and *P. aurelia*
- *Paramecium* culture medium
- Uncooked rice
- Three 200 mL deep Petri dishes
- 50 mL graduated cylinder
- Parafilm
- Pipette

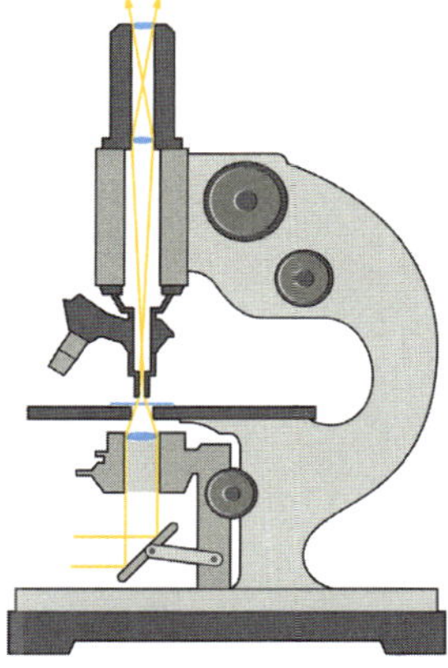

FIGURE 1 A light microscope

Method

1 Select the hypothesis to be tested.
2 Into each of three clean Petri dishes place 30 mL of distilled water, 20 mL of *Paramecium* culture medium and 6 grains of uncooked rice (to maintain the bacterial culture).
3 Into Petri dish 1, transfer 30 mL *Paramecium caudatum* from the pure culture.
4 Into Petri dish 2, transfer 30 mL *Paramecium aurelia* from the pure culture.
5 Into Petri dish 3, transfer 30 mL *Paramecium caudatum* and 30 mL *Paramecium aurelia* from the pure cultures.
6 Cover each dish with Parafilm.
7 Place all Petri dishes on a protected bench with a stable temperature (e.g. 24°C).
8 Design a sampling method that will allow you to count the relative number of organisms in each Petri dish. Remember that sampled organisms must remain part of the population.
9 Using your sampling method, every 2 days record the relative number of each type of *Paramecium* in each Petri dish. Record your results in Table 1. Repeat this over a 3 week period. At the time of counting, squirt in an additional 10 mL of distilled water.

Results

TABLE 1 Relative number of each *Paramecium* culture

Paramecium	1	3	5	7	9	11	13	15	17	19	21
P. caudatum											
P. aurelia											
P. caudatum											
P. aurelia											

1 Plot the results on a linear graph.

Discussion

Write a discussion of your results, including the following points:

- an appraisal (advantages and disadvantages) of the sampling technique
- a comparison of the population sizes of each *Paramecium* sp. in single culture and in mixed culture
- an explanation for the addition of extra fresh water at each sampling date and why it was 'squirted'
- interpretation of the graph(s)
- interpretation of the data in relation to the hypothesis tested
- limiting factors in the experiment.

Conclusion

Write a brief summary of your findings.

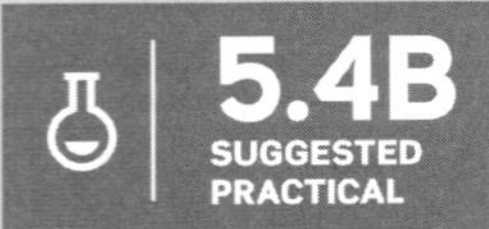

Relationship between predator and prey

Carry out a longitudinal study of keystone species and relevant ecological interactions.

Source: *Biology 2019 v1.2 General Senior Syllabus* © Queensland Curriculum & Assessment Authority

Aim

To analyse the feeding relationship between two pond organisms

Materials

- Six 500 mL beakers
- Pipette
- Rich culture of *Daphnia*
- Six damselfly nymphs
- Pond water
- Six short sticks

Method

1 Place 400 mL of pond water into each of the six beakers and label them A to F.

2 Put a short stick and one damsel fly nymph into each beaker and leave for about 10 minutes.

3 Using the pipette, transfer into beaker:

A 5 *Daphnia*
B 10 *Daphnia*
C 15 *Daphnia*
D 20 *Daphnia*
E 30 *Daphnia*
F 50 *Daphnia*

Results

1 After 40 minutes, remove the damselfly nymph from each beaker and count the number of *Daphnia* remaining. Record the results in Table 1.

2 Pool the class results. Use these to calculate the average number of *Daphnia* remaining in each beaker after 40 minutes of predation. Record this in Table 1.

TABLE 1 Number of *Daphnia* after predation

Sample	Number of *Daphnia* remaining
A	
B	
C	
D	
E	
F	
Class average	

3 Plot the average number of *Daphnia* eaten (vertical axis) against the number of *Daphnia* present at the start of the experiment.

Discussion

Write a discussion of your results, including the following points:

- the relationship between the rate of predation and the density of the prey
- the homeostatic control of populations.

Conclusion

Write a brief summary of your findings.

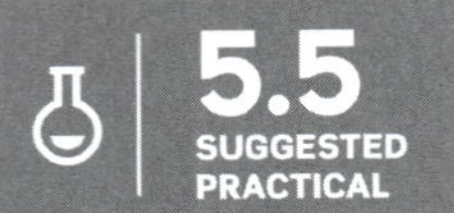

Population study of yeast

Measure the population of microorganisms in petri dishes to observe carrying capacity.

Source: *Biology 2019 v1.2 General Senior Syllabus* © Queensland Curriculum & Assessment Authority

Aims

1 To use a sampling technique to determine density changes in a yeast population
2 To compare the number of yeast cells present at the start of the yeast population with the number present during later time intervals
3 To calculate and graph the actual number of cells present in the yeast population

Materials

- Microscope
- Haemocytometer slide
- Cover slip
- Teat pipettes
- 2% sucrose solution (nutrient medium)
- Suspension of brewer's yeast
- 50 mL graduated cylinder
- 250 mL conical flask
- Cotton wool stopper

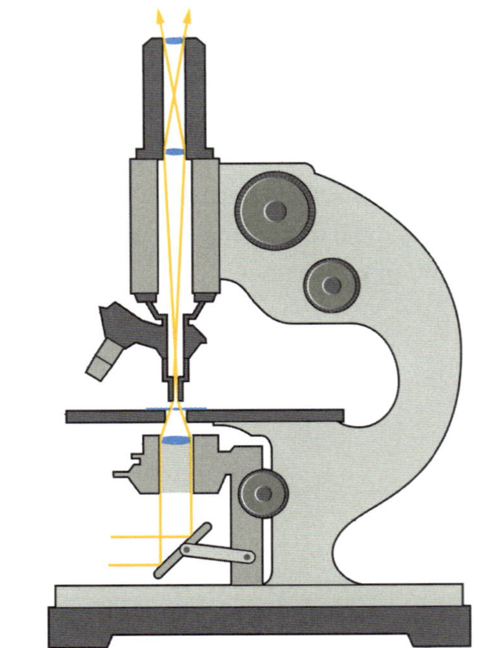

FIGURE 1 A light microscope

Method

1 Using a clean graduated cylinder, measure 50 mL of nutrient medium and pour it into the 250 mL conical flask.
2 Swirl the flask containing the yeast suspension. When the yeast is well mixed, collect some of the suspension with a clean teat pipette. Add one drop of the yeast suspension to the nutrient medium in the conical flask.
3 Plug the conical flask with cotton wool (this allows air movement only) and place in a warm cupboard.
4 Using the haemocytometer slide, take yeast cell counts twice daily over a minimum of 3 days. Before taking a sample, swirl the flask to ensure even distribution of yeast cells. Place 1 drop of the sample onto the slide. Count the number of yeast cells in four of the selected grid squares. Record the total number of cells and total count area in Table 1. Repeat with a second and third sample, recording the results in Tables 2 and 3. Average the number of cells for that area. To ensure comparability, record any yeast bud as a cell.

5 Calculate the number of yeast cells per unit volume (your total grid area × 0.1 mm) for each sampling time. Record your calculations in Table 1.

6 Calculate the number of yeast cells per cm^3 for each sampling time. Record your calculations in Table 1.

Results

TABLE 1 Population of yeast cells for sample 1

Sample 1	Number of yeast cells					
	0 h	24 h	48 h	72 h	96 h	120 h
Square 1						
Square 2						
Square 3						
Square 4						
Total count						
Average for area						
Cells per unit volume						
Cells per cm^3						

TABLE 2 Population of yeast cells for sample 2

Sample 2	Number of yeast cells					
	0 h	24 h	48 h	72 h	96 h	120 h
Square 1						
Square 2						
Square 3						
Square 4						
Total count						
Average for area						
Cells per unit volume						
Cells per cm^3						

TABLE 3 Population of yeast cells for sample 3

Sample 3	Number of yeast cells					
	0 h	24 h	48 h	72 h	96 h	120 h
Square 1						
Square 2						
Square 3						
Square 4						
Total count						
Average for area						
Cells per unit volume						
Cells per cm^3						

1 Plot the results on linear graph paper with time on the horizontal axis and number of yeast cells per cm^3 on the vertical axis. Alternatively, you can use Microsoft Excel to plot the graphs.

2 Plot the results on semi-logarithmic paper (i.e. graph paper in which the vertical axis only has been calibrated on a logarithmic scale).

Discussion/Conclusion

Write a discussion of your results, including the following points:

- the advantages and disadvantages of the sampling technique
- a description of the shape of the curve in the linear graph
- an explanation of any phases shown in the graph
- the period of exponential growth
- an explanation for any differences in the shape of the curve between the linear and semi-logarithmic graphs
- the purpose of using semi-logarithmic graph paper in investigations of this type
- possible environmental factors that might have affected the population growth
- the possible results after several weeks. Justify your answer.

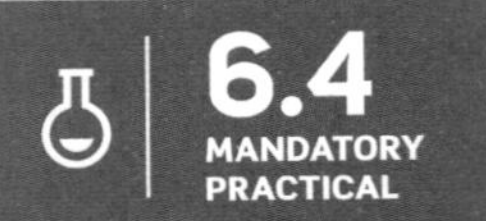

Appraisal of an ecological surveying technique

Select and appraise an ecological surveying technique to analyse species diversity between two spatially variant ecosystems of the same classification (e.g. disturbed or undisturbed dry sclerophyll forest).

Source: *Biology 2019 v1.2 General Senior Syllabus* © Queensland Curriculum & Assessment Authority

Aims

1 To design an experiment to survey two ecosystems of the same classification that are spatially variant, e.g. disturbed (e.g. roadside) versus undisturbed dry sclerophyll forest; grassland sprayed for weeds compared with that not sprayed; or a recently burnt area of woodland versus an unburnt area
2 To select and appraise the technique(s) used to survey the areas
3 To carry out the survey
4 To analyse the species diversity at each site

Method

1 Select the ecosystems that are going to be investigated.
2 Consider the factors needed to be incorporated in the survey.
3 Taking the ecosystem into consideration, consider the range of sampling techniques available and which would be most suitable for the locality, e.g. quadrats, line transect, belt transect.
4 Appraise each technique to determine the most appropriate for the ecosystem you are testing. Include safety aspects of moving around the terrain and ways to minimise harm to the local plants and wildlife. This can be completed when you fill out your risk assessment for this practical.
5 Write the sequence of steps used in the survey. Include enough detail so that the survey could be repeated by another scientist at a later date.

6 Complete the survey according to your method. Note any variations that may have been necessary due to environmental conditions.

7 Calculate species diversity in each locality.

Results

Species diversity:

Discussion

Write a discussion of your results, including the following points:

- justification for the survey technique(s)
- problems (and the solutions used) that might have arisen during the surveys related to the technique(s)
- possible improvements that could be made to the survey technique(s)
- the level of species diversity in the two localities
- suggest possible correlations (including explanations) between the environmental conditions and the relative species diversity between the two tested sites.

Conclusion

Write a brief summary of your findings.

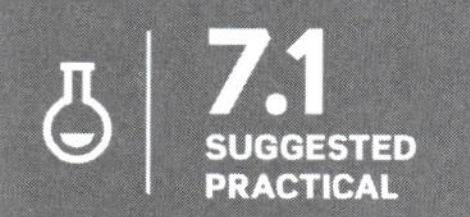

Extraction of strawberry DNA

Extract DNA from strawberries, kiwifruit or wheat germ.

Source: *Biology 2019 v1.2 General Senior Syllabus* © Queensland Curriculum & Assessment Authority

Aim

To extract DNA from strawberry cells

Materials

- 4 large strawberries
- Knife
- Chopping board
- Blender or Bamix®
- 250 mL beakers
- 500 mL beaker or suitable container (for ice bath)
- 100 mL measuring cylinder
- 10 mL measuring cylinder (to measure protease enzyme)
- Hot plate (do not use a Bunsen burner)
- Thermometer
- Timer
- Ethanol (ice cold)
- 'Lux' soap flakes
- Electronic balance
- Protease enzyme
- 'Chux®' cloth
- Glass rod with hook on the end
- Specimen bottle

Method

1. Cut four large strawberries, using a sharp knife and cutting board, into very small pieces.
2. Add the strawberry pieces to the blender with 100 mL of warm tap water. Blend for 10–15 seconds.
3. Place the blended strawberries and water in a 250 mL beaker. Add 3 g of 'Lux' soap flakes and stir.
4. Heat the mixture to 65°C and hold at this temperature for 8 minutes, stirring gently.
5. Cool the mixture to 40°C by running cold tap water over the outside of the beaker for 2 minutes and then placing it in an ice-water bath (use a 400 mL beaker) until the required temperature is reached. Stir gently during the cooling process. *Cooling the strawberry mixture slows down the breakdown of DNA.*
6. Add 5 mL of protease enzyme and stir gently for 5 minutes.
7. Filter the mixture through a double thickness of 'Chux' cloth into a 100 mL beaker. Squeeze the material in the 'Chux' cloth to get all the juice out of it.
8. Place 10 mL of the liquid strawberry filtrate into the specimen bottle.
9. Add 10 mL of ice-cold ethanol to the specimen bottle, pouring slowly and carefully down the side of the specimen bottle so that the ice-cold ethanol sits on top of the filtrate. It might be easier to add the ice-cold ethanol to the strawberry filtrate using a pipette.
10. Let it sit for 2 or 3 minutes. The DNA is not soluble in ethanol and should precipitate out of solution near the boundary between the strawberry filtrate and the ethanol.

FIGURE 1 A strawberry

11 Gently swirl the DNA using the narrow glass rod with a hook on the end. Swirl the glass rod so the hook is in the strawberry filtrate just below the ethanol and gently lift it up through the ethanol. DNA should be on the glass rod near the hook. Repeat this swirling action several times to accumulate a good amount of DNA. (DNA looks like white mucus – the clearer it is, the fewer impurities are present.).

Discussion

Write a discussion of your results including the following points:

- reasons for blending the strawberries
- the effects of heating the strawberry mixture and the reasons for maintaining the heat at 65°C
- methods of removing proteins that might contaminate the DNA.

Conclusion

Write a brief summary of your findings.

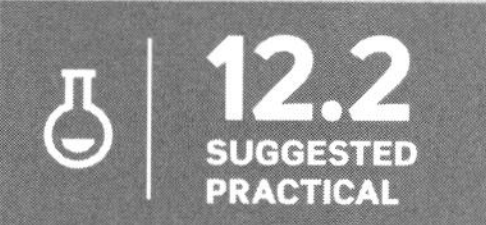

Performing a bacterial transformation

Perform a bacterial transformation.

Source: *Biology 2019 v1.2 General Senior Syllabus* © Queensland Curriculum & Assessment Authority

Aim

To use bacterial transformation techniques to mass-produce surface proteins from a virus

Materials

- 1 mL Pasteur pipette or micropipette
- 1.5 mL Eppendorf tubes
- Warm water bath
- Ice bath
- Stopwatch
- Bacterial hockey stick spreaders or inoculating loops
- Solutions:
  - 'calcium chloride' – mock solution (1 tablespoon sodium chloride to 1 L water; include 1 drop of blue food dye in 1 L of water)
  - 'bacterial suspension' – mock solution (1/2 teaspoon corn flour to 1 L water)
  - 'plasmid suspension' – mock solution (1 drop yellow food dye to 1 L water)
  - 'antibiotic-embedded nutrient agar plates' – plain agar/gelatin plates.

Method

1. Transfer 0.3 mL of bacterial solution to an Eppendorf tube using a pipette. Mark the lid of the tube 'X' (indicating the experimental vial).
2. Using a clean pipette, transfer 0.3 mL of calcium chloride into the experimental vial.
3. Push the lid down firmly and mix by flicking the base of the tube gently. Place the experimental vial in an ice bath and chill for 2 minutes.
4. Using a clean pipette, transfer 0.3 mL of plasmid suspension to the experimental vial.
5. Place the experimental vial into a warm water bath (40–50°C) for 1 minute.
6. After 1 minute, place the experimental vial into the ice bath for 2 minutes.
7. Using a clean pipette, transfer 0.5 mL of plasmid/bacterial solution to an antibiotic-embedded nutrient agar plate. Spread using either a sterile hockey stick spreader or an inoculating loop (your teacher will demonstrate this technique).
8. Seal the plate and label with the date, initials and type of growth media used. ('A+ agar' is usually used for antibiotic-embedded nutrient agar plates.) Once plates are inoculated, they would normally be stored in an incubator at 37°C for 48 hours.

Results

Describe the results at 48 hours.

Discussion

1 At each of the following steps, describe what is happening at the micro-scale.

a Adding the calcium chloride to the bacterial suspension

b Placing the experimental tube in alternating warm/ice baths

c Incubating the agar plates for 48 hours

2 Describe the characteristics of the bacterial colonies that have grown on the agar plate.

3 Research and explain why agar plates are incubated upside down.

4 The bacterial colonies on the agar plate will be grown on in 500 L fermentation tanks. These will produce large volumes of the viral surface protein ready to be turned into vaccine. List the other components that will need to be added to the fermentation tanks to produce the vaccine.

Conclusion

Write a brief summary of your findings.

Gel electrophoresis

Interpret DNA profiles from gel electrophoresis (either laboratory or simulation based).

Source: *Biology 2019 v1.2 General Senior Syllabus* © Queensland Curriculum & Assessment Authority

Aim

1 To use restriction enzymes to cut lambda DNA into fragments
2 To use gel electrophoresis to separate the DNA fragments according to size

Context

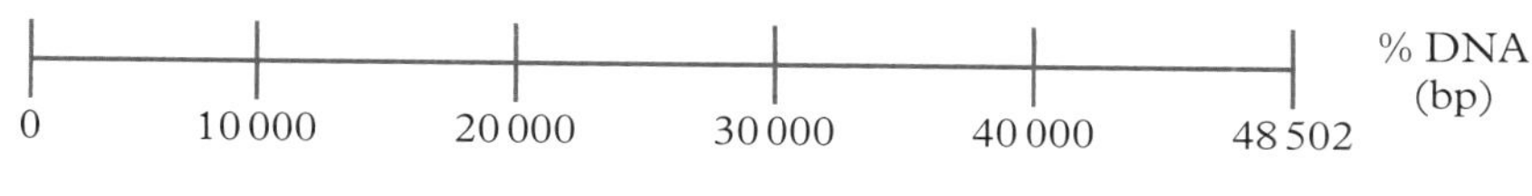

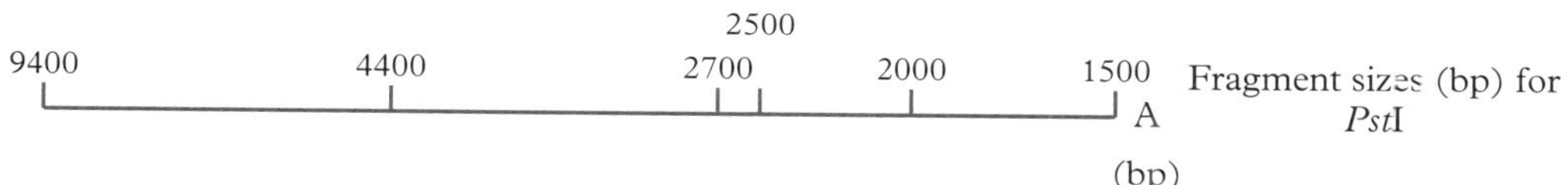

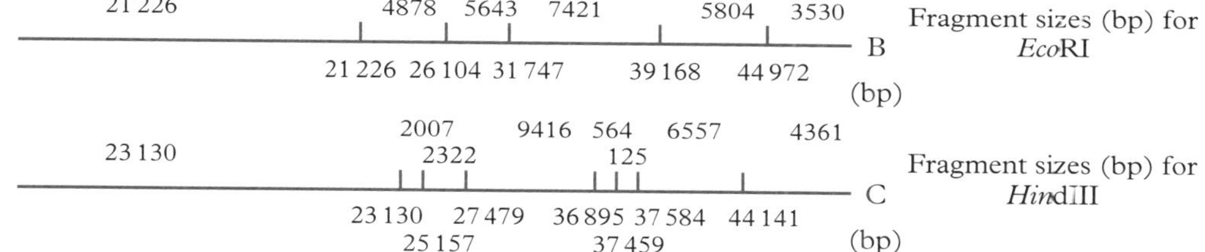

FIGURE 1 Restriction enzyme cutting sites of lambda DNA

Materials

- 25 μL TBE buffer for digestion
- 30 mL TBE buffer for gel electrophoresis
- 10 μL DNA ladder (with loading dye)
- 20 μL lambda DNA
- 1 μL *Hind*III restriction enzyme (on ice)
- 1 μL *Pst*I restriction enzyme (on ice)
- 1 μL *Eco*RI restriction enzyme (on ice)
- One 20 μL micropipette
- Pipette tips
- Four micro test tubes
- Permanent marker
- Floating (foam) rack for the micro test tubes
- 37°C water bath
- Stopwatch

- Eight 10 μL aliquots of loading dye
- 2% agarose gel with 2 μL SYBRTM Safe DNA stain added
- Gel electrophoresis chamber (measurements are based on a blueGel™ unit)

Method

1 Use a fresh pipette tip to place 4 μL of lambda DNA into each micro test tube.
2 Use the permanent marker to label one test tube 'C' (control). Use a fresh tip to add 6 μL of the buffer to this micro test tube.
3 Use a fresh tip to add 5 μL of buffer to the remaining three micro test tubes.
4 Use the permanent marker to label a test tube 'H'. Use a fresh tip to add 1 μL of *Hind*III to the micro test tube.
5 Use the permanent marker to label a test tube 'P'. Use a fresh tip to add 1 μL of *Pst*I to the micro test tube.
6 Use the permanent marker to label a test tube 'E'. Use a fresh tip to add 1 μL of *Eco*RI to the micro test tube.
7 Use your finger to gently 'flick' the base of each micro test tube. This mixes all the components of the DNA digestion. Tap the base of each test tube (or spin in a microcentrifuge) to collect the liquid on the base of the micro test tube.
8 Place all four tubes in the floating foam rack and incubate in the 37°C water bath for 30 minutes.
Note: The contents can be stored in the refrigerator overnight after step 8.
9 Use a fresh pipette tip to add 2 μL of the sample loading dye to each micro test tube. Mix the dye through the sample by 'flicking' the base of the test tube with your finger. Tab the base of the test tube on the bench (or pulse spin with a microcentrifuge) to collect the contents on the bottom of the tube.
10 Place the prepared gel into the gel electrophoresis chamber so that the wells are located at the negative anode. Add the TBE buffer until it just covers the gel.
11 Use a fresh micropipette tip to add 10 μL of sample from the contents of each of the micropipette test tubes into individual wells in the electrophoresis gel. Add 10 μL of the DNA ladder to another well of the electrophoresis gel. Record the order in which each sample was added to each well.
12 Carefully place the lid on the electrophoresis gel. Connect the electrical leads to the ports of the electrophoresis chamber (the negative is connected to the end closest to the DNA samples).
13 Turn on the power and run the gel for approximately 20–30 minutes (100 V).
14 Use a fluorescent green light to examine the location (and length) of the DNA fragments.

Discussion

Answer the following.

1 Explain why the DNA samples must be loaded at the negative end of the electrophoresis gel.

____

____

____

2 Describe the origin of restriction enzymes.

____

____

____

3 Identify the evidence that shows that each enzyme cuts the lambda DNA at different locations.

4 Use Figure 1 above to determine how many fragments of DNA will be found in:

a C (the uncut control)

b H (cut with *Hind*III)

c P (cut with *Pst*I)

d E (cut with *Eco*RI).

5 Calculate the number of times the sequence GAATC (recognition site of *Eco*RI) occurs in lambda DNA.

6 Describe any correlation between the results of your gel and the expected results.

Conclusion

Write a brief summary of your findings.

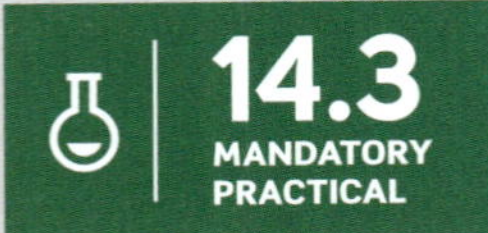

14.3 MANDATORY PRACTICAL Changes in the gene pool due to selection pressure

Analyse genotypic changes for a selective pressure in a gene pool (modelling can be based on laboratory work or computer simulation).

Source: *Biology 2019 v1.2 General Senior Syllabus* © Queensland Curriculum & Assessment Authority

Aims

1 To model a gene pool through successive generations
2 To determine the effects on the gene pool over successive generations under varying selection pressures
3 To compare the effects of different selection pressures on the gene pool
4 To discuss limitations of evolutionary modelling

Materials

- Approximately 100 plastic discs of three different colours in a black cloth bag:
- Colour 1 = homozygous dominant
- Colour 2 = heterozygous (one side marked with an X to indicate the allele for the dominant trait)
- Colour 3 = homozygous recessive

Method

A Assumption 1: There is no selection pressure to change the gene pool.

1 Decide which disc colour represents each genotype. Record your decision in Table 1.

TABLE 1 Genotypes and their colours

Genotype	Colour
Homozygous dominant	
Heterozygous	
Homozygous recessive	

2 Place four of each colour disc in the bag.
3 Withdraw two discs (parents) randomly. Record the parents and determine the genotype of the four possible offspring (in a Punnett square). Record your results in a table similar to the one below. Repeat until all 'parents' have mated, equalling six matings with 24 offspring. **Note:** The table below is an example of how to set up your own table. You will need a full page of your own paper to write down your results.

TABLE 2 Assumption 1 – Parents and their offspring

Genotype of parent A	Genotype of parent B	Genotypes of offspring			
		1	2	3	4

Genotype of parent A	Genotype of parent B	Genotypes of offspring			
		1	2	3	4

4 From Table 2, count the number of each genotype of the offspring. Select the number of discs that represent these genotypes and place them in the bag (24 discs). Remember that parents die before the next mating.

5 Repeat steps 3 and 4 three more times.

TABLE 3 Numbers for each repeat

Generation	Number of parents	Number of matings	Number of offspring
1	12	6	24
2	24	12	48
3	48	24	96
4	96	48	192

6 Determine the ratio of genotypes in generation 4. Record the results. Compare this ratio with that of the original population.

____

____

____

B Assumption 2: Selection pressure acts against homozygous recessives.

1 Place four of each of two colours of discs in the bag (excluding the homozygous recessive discs).

2 Withdraw two discs (parents) randomly. Record the parents and determine the genotype of the four possible offspring (Punnett square). Record in a table similar to the one below. Repeat until all 'parents' have mated, equalling four matings with 16 offspring. **Note:** The table below is an example of how to set up your own table. You will need a full page of your own paper to write down your results.

TABLE 4 Assumption 2 – Parents and their offspring

Genotype of parent A	Genotype of parent B	Genotypes of offspring			
		1	2	3	4

Genotype of parent A	Genotype of parent B	Genotypes of offspring			
		1	2	3	4

3 From Table 4, count the number of each genotype of the offspring. Select the number of discs that represent these genotypes and place them in the bag (remembering to exclude the homozygous recessive offspring). Remember that parents die before the next mating.

4 Repeat steps 2 and 3 three more times. (Record the results for each repeating step.)

5 Determine the ratio of genotypes in generation 4. Record the results. Compare this ratio with that of the original population.

C Assumption 3: Selection pressure acts against heterozygotes.

1 Place eight of the heterozygote coloured discs in the bag.

2 Withdraw two discs (parents) randomly. Record the parents and determine the genotype of the four possible offspring (a Punnett square). Record in a table similar to the one below. Repeat until all 'parents' have mated, equalling four matings with 16 offspring. **Note:** The table below is an example of how to set up your own table. You will need a full page of your own paper to write down your results.

TABLE 5 Assumption 3 – Parents and their offspring

Genotype of parent A	Genotype of parent B	Genotypes of offspring			
		1	2	3	4

3 From Table 5, count the number of each genotype of the offspring. Select the number of discs that represent these genotypes and place them in the bag (remembering to exclude the offspring). Remember that parents die before the next mating.

4 Repeat steps 2 and 3 three more times. (Record the results for each repeating step.)

5 Determine the ratio of genotypes in generation 4. Record the results. Compare this ratio with that of the original population.

Discussion

Write a discussion of your results, including the following points:

- the validity of the assumptions in relation to a 'real' population
- the action of selection pressures in changing the gene pool for a specific species characteristic over time; give reasons for your decision
- whether, in this example, the changes would lead to clinal variation, formation of races, or speciation

Conclusion

Write a brief summary of your findings.

Answers

Chapter 1

DATA DRILL 1

1 15%

2

Sample	Balance (0.0 g, 0.00 g)
Small amounts of pharmaceutical compounds	0.00 g
Solid materials of a kilogram or more	0.0 g
A small marsupial	0.0 g
Wind-blown seeds	0.00 g

3 **a** yes, between minutes 70 and 85

b to allow steam to reach all parts of the load

EXPERIMENT EXPLORER 1

1
- Include aims, materials, methods, results, discussion and conclusions.
- Include tables, graphs and diagrams where appropriate.
- Check spelling and grammar.
- Don't use personal pronouns (I/we).
- Use dot points for materials.
- Include recommendations for further study if appropriate.

RESEARCH REVIEW 1

1 Student answers will vary depending on each student's reflection.

UNIT 3 WORD WIZARD

ABIOTIC	The non-living physical factors that affect an organism's ability to survive
DIVISION	Major classification group of the plants, fungi and plant-like protists
PHYLUM	Major classification group of the animal kingdom
POPULATION GROWTH	Increase in the size of a population in a particular habitat over time
PREDATION	Feeding of one organism (predator) on another (prey)
GENERALIST FEEDER	A heterotroph with a varied diet
STANDING CROP	Biomass of an organism at any particular moment
PIONEER SPECIES	Species of plants that colonise bare ground
SECONDARY FOREST	Climax forest formed due to secondary succession
PRODUCTIVITY	Amount of energy fixed in organic compounds; measured by increase in biomass per unit time
MUTUALISM	Necessary and positive association between two organisms
OMNIVORE	An organism that can utilise a range of nutrients; both herbivorous and carnivorous
BIODIVERSITY	The range of living organisms and their ecosystems
COMMUNITY	All the species that occupy a particular place at a particular time

Chapter 2

DATA DRILL 2

1 **a** lion and tiger: they have the lowest difference in the DNA hybridisation test

b

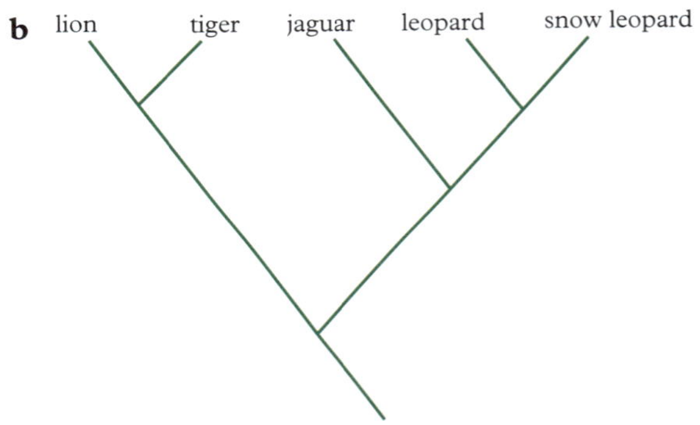

EXPERIMENT EXPLORER 2

1 **a** salinity, dissolved oxygen, temperature, pH

b pH of soil, temperature, light

RESEARCH REVIEW 2

1 Simplify jargon, slow down on difficult concepts, use diagrams for difficult concepts, use key words/ideas/buzz words that you want the audience to remember, use visual aids, ask questions and get the audience involved.

EXAM EXCELLENCE 2

1 B

2 D

3 D

4 A

5 C

6 a

Domain	Archaea	Bacteria	Eukarya			
Kingdom	Archaebacteria	Eubacteria	Protista	Fungi	Plantae	Animalia
Characteristics	Distinguished on the basis of rRNA and cell wall composition					
Cell type	Prokaryote	Prokaryote	Eukaryote	Eukaryote	Eukaryote	Eukaryote
Chloroplasts	Absent	Absent	Present in some forms	Absent	Present	Absent
Mode of nutrition	Heterotrophs or chemosynthetic autotrophs	Heterotrophs that require oxygen or autotrophs (photosynthesis)	Photosynthesis or heterotrophic or combination of both	Heterotrophic by absorption	Autotroph	Heterotrophic by ingestion
Multi-cellularity	Absent	Absent	Present except in yeasts	Present except in yeasts	Present	Present
Locomotion	Absent	Absent in most	Absent	Absent	Absent	Present
Nervous system	Absent	Absent	Absent	Absent	Absent	Present except in sponges

b Fungi do not have chloroplasts and their cell walls are different.

7 a to be able to identify and communicate their usefulness to others

b There are many tribes in Australia and, due to distance and differences in language, they would have had different names for the same organisms. Australian scientists are required to follow the 'worldwide' classification system.

8 a Usually sterile, it may have characteristics (behavioural and anatomical) of both parents, but these are not predictable.

b A liger would not have a species name as its offspring would not be able to breed, and the ability to have fertile offspring is one of the characteristics that determines a species.

9 a Homologous structures have the same internal structure, but different functions. Analogous structures have a different internal structure, but the same function.

b i homologous

ii analogous

iii analogous (the structure is different but has the same purpose – forward motion)

10 a type of snake, length, colour, location in airport

b unknown snake species – possibly from overseas

c compete with native snakes for food, introduce new diseases, prey on different species

Chapter 3

DATA DRILL 3

1 Because the Simpson's Diversity Index for community B (0.45) is higher than that for community A (0.36), community B is considered to be more diverse than community A.

2 1620 at Warrego River, 310 at Lake Bindegolly

EXPERIMENT EXPLORER 3

1

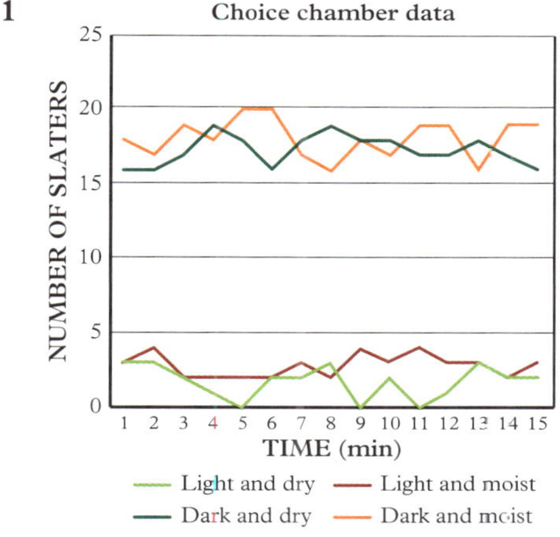

RESEARCH REVIEW 3

1 Clean layout; not too many words; can be read from 1 m away; simple and effective diagrams; should include title, authors, references, aim, research question, method, results, discussion and conclusion.

EXAM EXCELLENCE 3

1 D

2 D

3 A

4 D

5 B

6 The optimum range is the level at which an organism can best survive; the tolerance range includes the optimum range and the zones of physiological stress, where organisms can survive but will not function as efficiently.

7

	Freshwater	Marine
Movement of water between environment and organisms due to dissolved salts	Water moves into organisms' cells	Water moves out of organisms' cells
Depth	Shallower	Deeper
Water pressure	Less	More
Water temperature variability	More variable	Less variable
Variety of organisms	Less varied	More varied

8 **a** wet sclerophyll → dry sclerophyll → arid saltbush

b woodland or scrub

9 **a** Burlese–Tullgren funnel, pitfall traps

b pitfall traps

10 Polyps and algae live in symbiosis → increasing water temperatures → polyps reject algae → coral becomes white.

Chapter 4

DATA DRILL 4

1 **a**

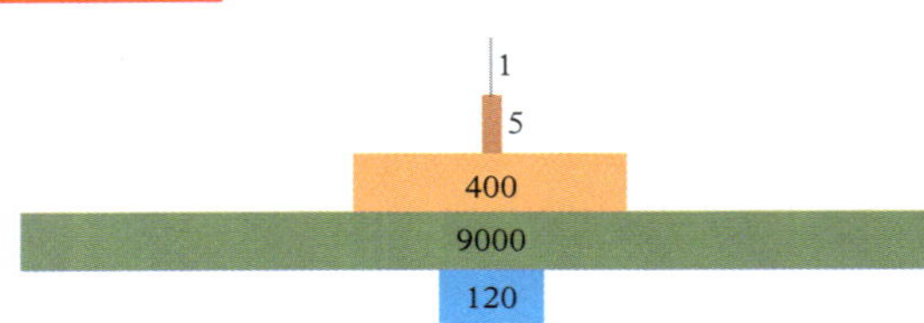

b

Organism	Biomass
Flowering plants/trees	120 000 kg
Butterflies/moths	45 kg
Insectivorous bats	10 kg
Snakes	5 kg
Owl	1.5 kg

c

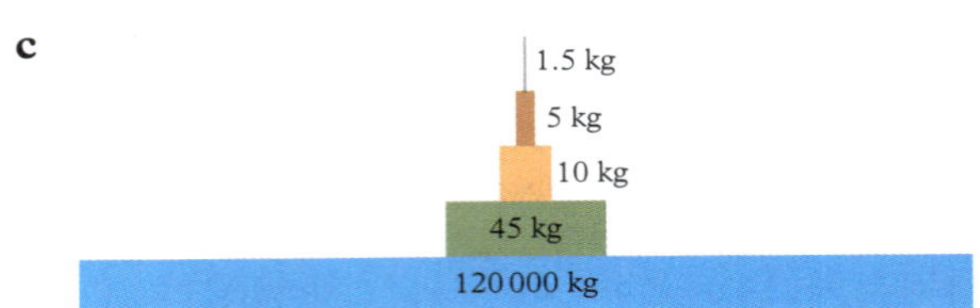

EXPERIMENT EXPLORER 4

1

Guidelines	Why this is necessary
Use SI units only.	This keeps data measurements constant.
Cannot change a hypothesis once the data are collected.	A hypothesis is based on past research rather than new data and shouldn't be changed.
Where possible, take multiple samples (two or more) or run multiple tests on the same sample.	Multiple samples and multiple tests help reduce errors and outliers by averaging the samples.
Experiments should be repeatable under similar conditions.	Repeatability shows that the method is sound and produces similar results, lending more credibility to the study.
Results should be presented on a table or graph.	Trends are easier to observe when presented graphically.
Experimental positive and negative controls should be used where possible.	Positive and negative controls help to ensure the equipment and reagents used, and the method followed, are working as they should be.
Only change one variable at a time.	This helps to determine exactly what is causing the change in the dataset.

RESEARCH REVIEW 4

1 – Pesticides decrease invertebrates.

– Aphids affect monoculture crops.

– Reducing pesticide use helps increase the abundance of arthropod predators.

– This reduces aphid numbers.

2

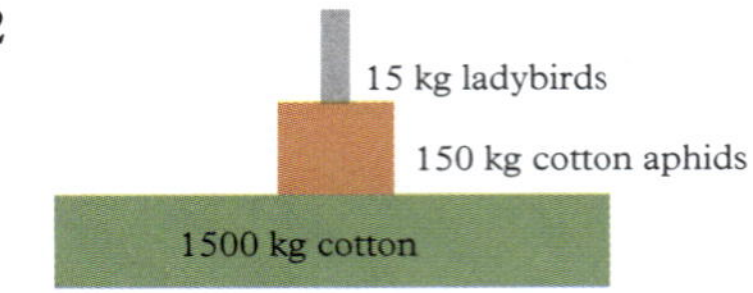

EXAM EXCELLENCE 4

1 B

2 B

3 A

4 D

5 D

6 a A decline in the native mouse population would lead to an increase in the grass population.

b A decline in the native mouse population would lead to a decline in the snake population.

7 a

1 octopus
100 fish
50 000 zooplankton
1 000 000 algae

b

1 kg
5 kg
25 kg
500 kg

c

2 units energy (1 lost as heat)
10 units energy (5 lost as heat)
500 units energy (100 lost as heat)
10 000 units energy (7500 lost as heat)

8

Reservoir pool	Nutrients	Cycling pool
Artesian; glaciers; polar ice caps	Water	Transpiration – evaporation – precipitation – uptake
Metallic compounds	Oxygen	Photosynthesis – respiration
Fossils; peat; coal; oil and gas; trees	Carbon	Respiration – photosynthesis
Deep-sea sediments	Nitrogen	Nitrogen fixation – denitrification
Phosphate rock; deep-sea sediments	Phosphorus	Erosion – uptake –phosphatising

9 a respiration

b CO_2 dissolved in rainwater

c carbonates in sea

d CO_2 in air

10 a A keystone species is a species that has a disproportionately large effect on its environment relative to its abundance by maintaining local biodiversity within a community, either by controlling populations of other species that would otherwise dominate the community or by providing critical resources.

b

Southern cassowary	Flying fox
• Large predator • Spreads seeds of over 238 plants	• Large populations controlling insect populations • Pollinators • Spread seeds

Chapter 5

DATA DRILL 5

1 a

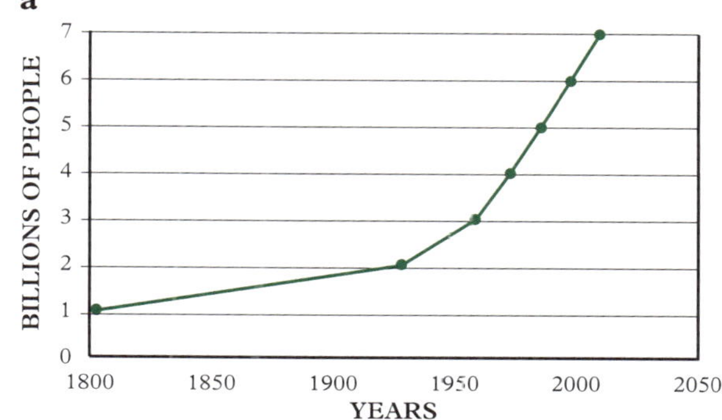

b i mass vaccination programs – increase population

ii war – decreases population

iii famine and drought – decrease population

iv contraception – decreases population

EXPERIMENT EXPLORER 5

1 Fruit flies in laboratories grow more consistently than in the wild. Scientists in a lab can remove many of the factors limiting the growth of a population in the wild (food, space, etc.).

2 The two environments would be relatively similar, as the temperature of a human digestive tract is quite constant. Nutrient availability would be more constant on the agar plate than in the digestive tract.

RESEARCH REVIEW 5

1 a

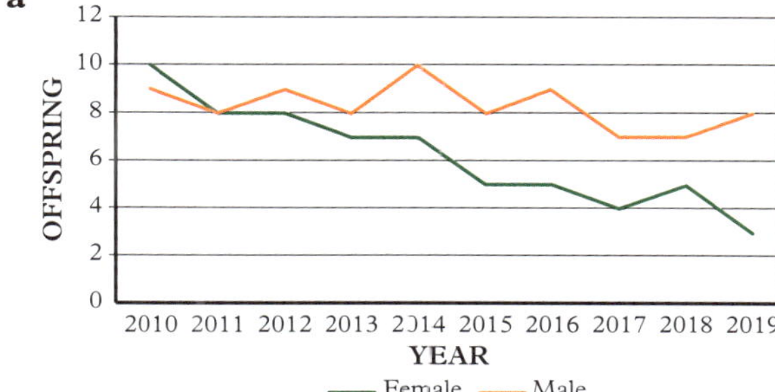

b There may have been an increased temperature due to the drought. This has increased the number of male-only nests, while decreasing the number of female-only nests. The drop in water level has reduced the territory, size and the availability of food for some crocodiles, leading to fewer clutches of eggs being successfully hatched.

EXAM EXCELLENCE 5

1 B

2 B

3 C

4 B

5 B

6 a limited suitable nesting sites in Antarctica; less chance of predation; easier to find nest sites

b Coastal environments are restricted in size, so by evenly spacing nesting sites, the maximum number of nests can be fitted in.

7 Some potential positive effects are: increase in soil water, which could increase primary production; fertile silt deposition; seed dispersal. Some potential negative effects are: death of some organisms present in the ecosystem; erosion; weed seed dispersal.

8 a 87/day b C

9 a Some organisms display strategies of both *r*- and *K*-strategists.

b Trees, biofilms and sea turtles can all be large, long-lived and highly competitive (like *K*-strategists), but produce many unnurtured offspring (like *r*-strategists).

10 a increase in prey, increase in territory, increase in resources (e.g. fruiting trees)

b flooding event, bushfire, increase in predators

Chapter 6

DATA DRILL 6

1 a As the temperature decreases, the ratio of $^{18}O:^{16}O$ increases.

b As the concentration of CO_2 increases, the temperature increases.

2 CO_2 and methane concentration

EXPERIMENT EXPLORER 6

1 Example method for the research question, 'What is the effect of increased salinity on the growth of wheat seeds?'

- Plant wheat seeds in 10 pots with potting mix.
- Water with tap water until seeds have sprouted.
- Once they are 5 cm high, start watering with different concentrations of salt water:
  2 pots with tap water (control)
  2 pots with 1% salt water
  2 pots with 2% salt water
  2 pots with 3% salt water
  2 pots with 4% salt water.
- Over the next 3 weeks, record height and appearance daily.

2 Example of a hazard:

	Hazard 1
Step 1: Identify hazards. Are there any potential hazards in your method?	Broken glass
Step 2: Assess the risk. What is the likelihood of this hazard causing injury, illness or death?	Slight risk of injury
Step 3: Control the risk. How can you reduce the likelihood of this hazard causing injury, illness or death?	Provide gloves, dustpan and brush, and glass bin for clean up
Step 4: Reviewing risk controls. Risk assessments are regularly reviewed to see if the controls in place are working. How would you review your controls?	Keep a record of injuries involving broken glass. If high, review risk control.

RESEARCH REVIEW 6

1 reject – possibly biased, use of ambiguous terms (some, may)

2 accept – unbiased, precise data reported, scientifically accredited

EXAM EXCELLENCE 6

1 A

2 B

3 D

4 C

5 C

6 a i The development and change in plant communities over time, leading eventually from bare ground to a climax community.

ii Successive, natural changes in plant communities in an area where a previous community has been removed.

b Soil is already present, and seeds/soil organisms may be as well.

7 a Tropical rainforest gives way to deciduous forests, then to coniferous forests, and finally to tundra meadows near the poles.

b As altitude increases, the temperature decreases, and similarly when latitude changes from the equator to the poles, temperature decreases.

8 Pollen can give an indication of the species that existed in an area at a particular time, which can be used to construct historical vegetation maps of the area. The climatic conditions that would support such vegetation can be deduced.

9 Animals are able to travel via vegetation corridors to find new food and mates.

10

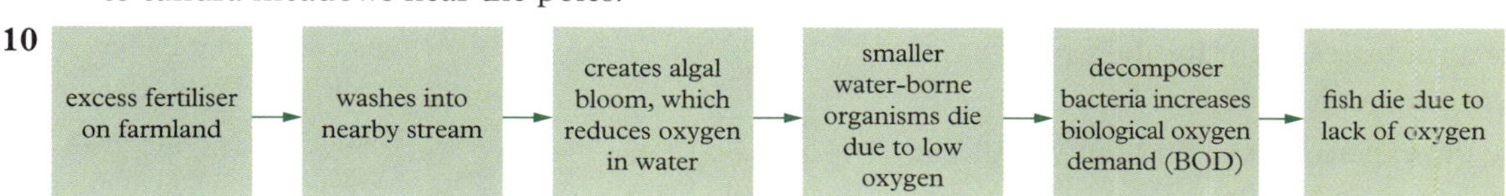

Unit 3 Practice assessment

DATA TEST

Dataset 1

Item 1:

a *N* males = 49 per km^2

b *N* females = 67 per km^2

c *N* total = 111 per km^2

Item 2:

Mating occurs in spring. Since the population size of males in October and November is calculated as zero, the males probably die after mating. This provides greater food resources for pregnant and lactating females – as evidenced by the higher number of females caught in traps during those months.

Item 3:

Approximately equal, as new males are recruited from births in the previous season

Dataset 2

Item 4:

Using canopy diameter:

Transect A: ~70% of the ground is 'covered' by the canopy.

Transect B: ~95% of the ground is 'covered' by the canopy.

Using the cross-wire tube:

Transect A: 5/10 sightings were leaves, 50% foliage coverage

Transect B: 7/10 sightings were leaves, 80% foliage coverage

Item 5:

Most eucalyptus trees have an open canopy that allows some light to pass. Therefore, the data collected using the cross-wire recordings are better.

Item 6:

Both are tall open forest.

Item 7:

Both transects contain *E. propinqua* and *E. drepanophylla*, and enough sunlight reaches ground level to support grasses and herbs. Both have the same soil type and ground profile, and are the same distance from the reservoir.

In Transect A, the proportion of *E. propinqua* to *E. drepanophylla* is 2:3, whereas in Transect B it is 4:2.

The trees in Transect A are more widely spaced than in Transect B, allowing more light penetration and growth of lantana and *Clerodendrum floribundum*.

Item 8:

Since a food supply and water are available in both areas, it could be that the bell miners require an understorey for survival, possibly as nesting sites.

Dataset 3

Item 9:

% heat loss of producers = 60%

% heat loss of carnivores = 80%

Carnivores use more energy. More metabolic reactions and a higher rate of respiration occur in carnivores than in plants.

Plants convert more solar energy into chemical energy during daylight (photosynthesis) than is used in respiration over a 24 hour period.

Item 10:

24%

STUDENT EXPERIMENT

Answers will vary based on the choice of modification, but students should make sure their experiment reflects the concept of 'measuring biomass'. Below is a set of points that each student should complete as they work through the Student experiment:

- Consider whether the aim needs to be changed after the modification.
- Write a research question.
- Research relevant literature if required for the modification.
- Complete a risk assessment for their new experiment and get it signed off by a teacher.
- Complete the experiment to find out whether it works.
- Collect enough data to answer their research question.
- Present their data in an appropriate scientific genre.
- Analyse any trends and limitations of the dataset.
- Draw conclusions from the new experiment and consider how it improves on the old experiment.

RESEARCH INVESTIGATION

Student answers will vary depending on the research question and resources selected.

A sample research question is:

'How does the timescale of natural climate changes on Earth differ from the current climate change?'

Resources should include information on previous climate shifts, current climate events and their possible links to human activities, etc.

UNIT 4 WORD WIZARD

DEOXYRIBONUCLEIC ACID (DNA)	A thread-like chain of nucleotides carrying the genetic instructions in a double-helix of antiparallel strands
HYDROCARBON	An organic compound comprising only carbon and hydrogen atoms
REDOX	A chemical reaction involving the transfer of electrons from one reactant to another
REDUCTION	A loss of electron from one atom to another
GENE	A region of DNA, made up of nucleotides, that encodes a function
HALF-CELL	Contains either the oxidation or reduction redox reaction
RIBONUCLEIC ACID (RNA)	A thread-like chain of nucleotides carrying the genetic instructions to form a protein in a cell
OXIDATION	A gain in electrons from an atom from another atom
DNA LIGASE	An enzyme that joins pieces of DNA
KETONE	A class of organic compound that contains a carbonyl functional group in the middle of the main chain
POLYSACCHARIDE	Multiple sugar monomers bonded together
AMINO ACID	An organic compound comprising an amine and a carboxyl functional group
MASS SPECTROMETRY	A technique used to determine the molecular weight of a compound
HABER PROCESS	A nitrogen fixation process to produce ammonia
BIODEGRADATION	Organisms able to breakdown a substance, such as plastic
MOLECULAR MANUFACTURING	The atomically precise placement of atoms or molecules in order to build larger molecular assemblies or molecular-based machines
MOLECULAR MACHINE	A molecular system with defined energy input that is capable of performing a useful function at the nanoscale
MITOSIS	nuclear division resulting in daughter cells having the same number and type of chromosomes as the parent cell
Y CHROMOSOME	male sex chromosome in vertebrates and some other animals
MUTATION	small permanent change in the DNA of an organism
KARYOTYPE	the number and visual appearance of the chromosomes in the cell nuclei of an organism or species

Chapter 7

RESEARCH REVIEW 7

1 a Neurobiology – the study of cells in the nervous system and the organisation of those cells into functioning circuits

b Entomology – the study of insects and their relationships to the environment

c Virology – the study of viruses and their interactions within a host

d Epigenetics – the study of non-genetic influences on gene expression

2 a the arising of life from non-living matter

b the measurements of bumps on the skull to predict personality traits

c a tiny human found in a sperm cell (preformationism)

EXAM EXCELLENCE 7

1 C

2 D

3 A

4 B

5 C

6

	DNA	RNA
Structure	Double stranded, composed of nucleotides A, T, G, C, deoxyribose sugar	Single stranded, composed of nucleotides A, U, G, C, ribose sugar
Function	Coding of proteins, passing on genetic information, reproduction of whole organism	Translating DNA code into proteins that are needed by the cell

7

DNA strand	ATGGTTTATTCCTCCC GCTTCAAAAACCGTCG ATCGCTAGCATAA
Complementary DNA strand	TACCAAATAAGGAGGG CGAAGTTTTTGGCAGC TAGCGATCGTATT
mRNA strand	UACCAAAUAAGGAGGG CGAAGUUUUUGGCAGC UAGCGAUCGUAUU

8 a DNA is wound around eight histone proteins. This complex is called a nucleosome.

b Uracil and thymine both bond with adenine: uracil in RNA and thymine in DNA.

9 a All; not all

b leading; lagging

10

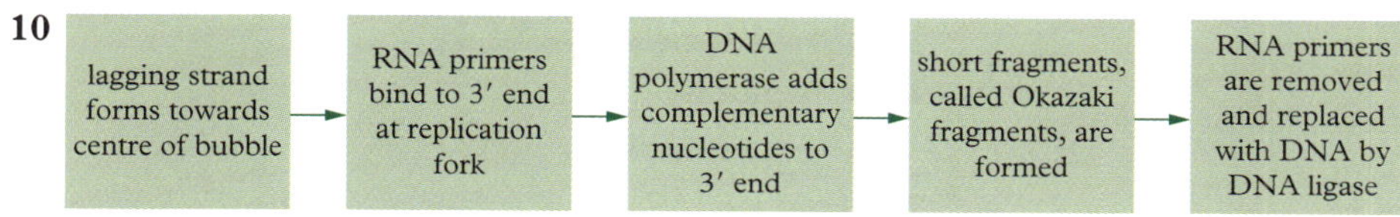

Chapter 8

RESEARCH REVIEW 8

1 a genetically modified food: not accurate as food is not coloured this way; an alternative more realistic image might be a double helix of DNA in one colour with a different coloured section being inserted into it

b genetically modified lemons: not accurate as lemons will not grow once picked; an alternative more realistic image might be an electrophoresis gel

EXAM EXCELLENCE 8

1 D

2 D

3 C

4 B

5 A

6 Anaphase I

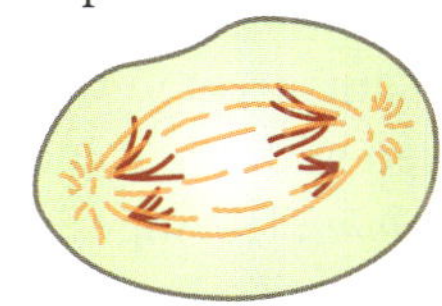

Anaphase I – one member of each homologous pair goes to the opposite end of the cell

Metaphase II

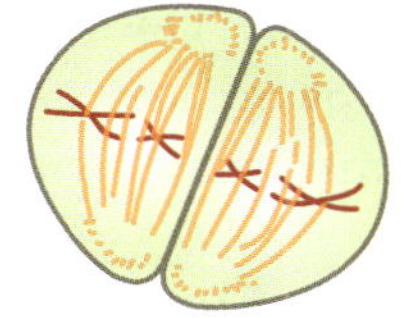

Metaphase II – chromosomes line up singly (as in mitosis)

Telophase II

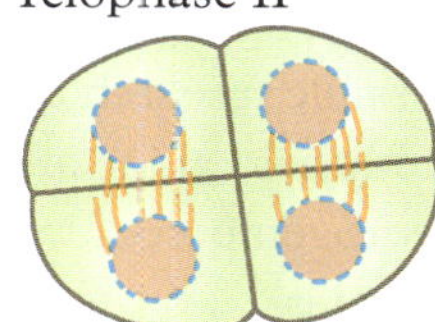

Telophase II – the chromosomes gather into nuclei, the cells divide

7 haploid as there are only 23 chromosomes, as found in the gametes

8 a secondary oocyte

9 **a** A genotype is the genetic code of an organism. The phenotype is the visible or expressed traits.

b A dominant trait is always expressed when present. A recessive trait is only expressed when there are two copies of the same allele.

10 This shows one chromosome having undergone double cross-over, and one undergoing single cross-over. Both must undergo double or single cross-over.

Chapter 9

RESEARCH REVIEW 9

1 Possible terms:
- phytoalexins – substances produced by plants that inhibit the growth of a pathogen
- oxidative burst – rapid release of hydrogen peroxide from cells
- cross-link – a process in which protein polymer chains form covalent bonds
- ppm – parts per million, a measure of concentration
- structural proteins – those proteins that provide structural frameworks for various tissues in organisms

2 Possible method:
- Collect four onion plants.
- Add a solution of hydrogen peroxide (30%) and acetic acid (100%) to two onion plants.
- Wait 3 days.
- Infect one of the onion plants treated with the solution and one untreated with the solution with *Phytophthora cinnamomi*, leaving the other two as controls.
- Wait 1 week.
- Observe, record and compare the health of the onion plants.

3 Possible research questions could be 'Does acetic acid alone affect plant growth?' and 'Does hydrogen peroxide added externally cross-link proteins?'

EXAM EXCELLENCE 9

1 D

2 A

3 B

4 D

5 C

6 **a** Transcription

b Translation

7 **a** Met-Ile-Ser-Tyr-Cys-Cys-Ala-stop

8 **a** Because the DNA is less tightly bound, it allows more efficient transcription to occur.

b These genes are more likely to be in a heterochromatin form, as the genes for placenta development are only needed during pregnancy and therefore do not need to be accessed as often.

9 a system of gene control outside of the DNA ('above the genome')

10 Methyl tags could be attached to the growth-promoting genes, inhibiting their transcription. Histones could be modified to deny access to growth-promoting genes by transcription factors.

Chapter 10

RESEARCH REVIEW 10

1 **a** genomic

b experimental

2 *Arabidopsis thaliana* (plant research), *Escherichia coli* (bacterial research).

EXAM EXCELLENCE 10

1 B

2 D

3 C

4 C

5 A

6 *BRCA1* codes for a protein that repairs DNA transcription errors. Without an effective *BRCA1* gene, the chances of mutations forming cancers increases.

7 a

Genetic disease	Caused by
Sickle cell anaemia	A point mutation in the gene for haemoglobin
Klinefelter syndrome	An extra X chromosome in a male (XXY)
Cri-du-chat syndrome	Deletion of top section of small arm of chromosome 5
Edwards syndrome	Trisomy of chromosome 18
Turner's syndrome	Only one X chromosome in a female
Cystic fibrosis	Mutation of the *CFTR* gene (a missense, frameshift or nonsense point mutation, frameshift mutation, or nonsense mutation; a splicing mutation; or deletion of a codon for an amino acid)

8 Males only have one X chromosome, whereas females have two.

9 a DNA replication, transcription and DNA packaging

b Repeated exposure to UV may mean DNA glycosylase can't repair all pyrimidine dimers.

10 A mutagen is a substance or factor that causes mutations in DNA, and a carcinogen is a mutagen that leads to the development of cancer.

Chapter 11

RESEARCH REVIEW 11

Student posters will vary considerably. Students should follow the guidelines listed.

EXAM EXCELLENCE 11

1 B

2 B

3 C

4 A

5 A

6 a The inheritance of alleles that does not follow Mendel's original discoveries, such as codominance and polygene traits.

b Mendel may not have published his paper, and our understanding of genetics would have fallen behind where it is today.

7 I^AI^A 25%, I^AI^B 25%, I^Ai 25%, I^Bi 25%

8 50%

9 As there is a range of heights rather than two distinct heights, the population shows a continuous variation, most likely caused by polygenes.

10

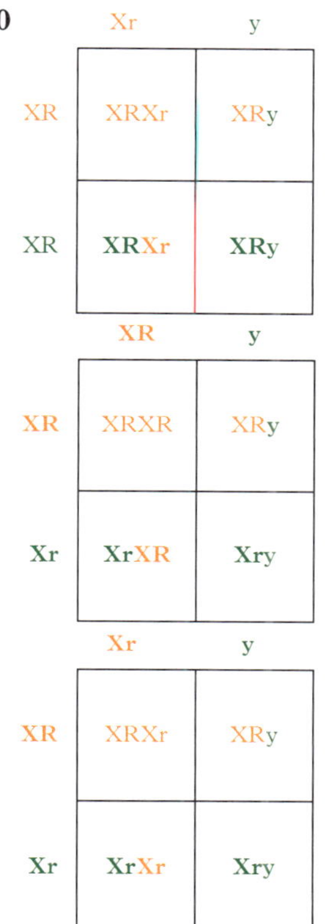

Chapter 12

RESEARCH REVIEW 12

1 *PG2* (*PGA2*) gene from tomatoes

2 FLAVR SAVR tomatoes are GMOs with their polygalacturonase-2a gene altered to prevent ripening of tomatoes.

3 BLAST is an excellent database for scientists. As scientists can easily upload their own sequences from their research, the database is kept current. The database produces an accession number that is typically used in a scientist's publication. However, the quality of the sequences submitted are at the discretion of the scientists.

EXAM EXCELLENCE 12

1 D
2 B
3 D
4 A
5 B
6 SCNT involves taking a nucleus containing diploid chromosomes from a somatic cell and placing it in an ovum cell that has had its nucleus removed; sexual fertilisation involves two haploid cells merging to form one diploid cell. Both processes result in a dividing diploid cell.
7 **a** Plasmids are smaller than bacterial chromosomes and contain fewer genes, but both are circular and found in the cytosol of bacteria.
b The recombined plasmid can move easily into bacteria, non-bacterial genes can be inserted into plasmids using the same restriction enzymes, and additional non-target genes can be added to monitor the success of the recombination.
8 Without a positive control in PCR, it would be difficult to assess whether the PCR process worked as intended.
9 **a** to compare nucleotide and protein sequences
b By comparing DNA sequences of different organisms, any evolutionary relationships between them can be identified to help build a phylogenetic tree.
10

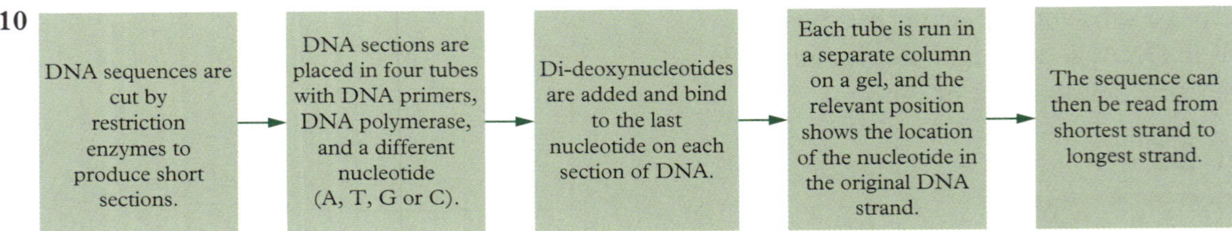

Chapter 13

RESEARCH REVIEW 13

1 Is *Archaeopteryx* the last common ancestor of birds and dinosaurs?
2 Resource 1 – Erickson GM, Rauhut OWM, Zhou Z-H, Turner AH, Inouye BD, et al. (2009) Was dinosaurian physiology inherited by birds? Reconciling slow growth in Designer *Archaeopteryx*. PLoS ONE 4: e7390.
Credible resource because it is published in a peer-reviewed journal.
Resource 2 – Wikipedia
Not a credible resource as it is not peer-reviewed. Anyone can update Wikipedia.

EXAM EXCELLENCE 13

1 C
2 C
3 C
4 A
5 B
6 patterns in geographic distribution of plants and animals, similarities in molecules and anatomy between organisms, similarities in DNA sequences between organisms, and fossil evidence
7 **a**

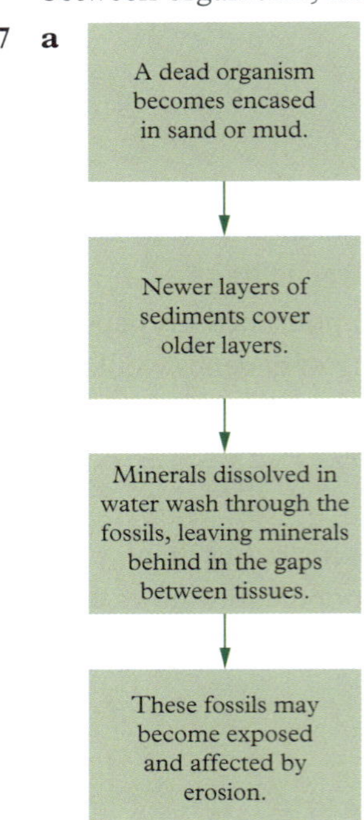

b Fur and skin do not fossilise well. Only hard body parts (e.g. bones and teeth) do.

8 A molecular clock is a gene with a known mutation rate. A conserved gene has a smaller chance of mutations than other genes, so it would appear to be a slower molecular clock.

9 a Mass extinction greatly reduces the populations of many species at once and leads to some species extinctions. Evolutionary radiation can occur after a mass extinction event and gives rise to new species.

b When the dinosaurs died out, there were vacant niches in the environment for mammals to move into.

10 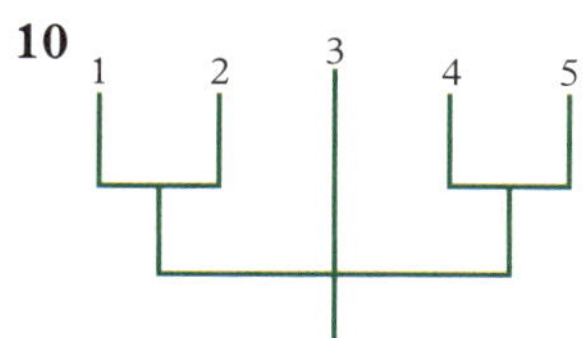

Chapter 14

RESEARCH REVIEW 14

1 a (Reznick et al., 2009)

b Reznick DN, Rocklefs RE. (2009) Darwin's bridge between microevolution and macroevolution. *Nature* 457:837–42.

2 Darwin C. (1859) *On the Origin of Species*. London: John Murray.

EXAM EXCELLENCE 14

1 A

2 A

3 D

4 C

5 B

6 Drought could lead to an increase in phenotype B due to those goats being able to extract more energy from the grass they can access.

7 large, small, small, large

8 The growth-inhibiting hormones and nitrogen inhibit the growth of fish, so a group that is separated off from the main population into a smaller lagoon can still survive and produce offspring, while using less resources and producing less waste. If the smaller population re-joins the larger population, they will still be able to grow to full size and breed.

9 homozygous dominant: 0.11; heterozygous: 0.44; homozygous recessive: 0.45

10 Natural selection is a large contributor to species extinctions. Extinctions occur when an environment changes and certain species prevail, while others struggle. Another example is when one organism evolves to have an advantageous feature or strategy (e.g. teeth, camouflage), allowing it to act as a more effective predator on other species.

Chapter 15

RESEARCH REVIEW 15

1 a No causal relationship.

b Causal relationship.

c Causal relationship.

EXAM EXCELLENCE 15

1 B

2 A

3 C

4 D

5 C

6 Behaviour makes the mimicry more believable to any predators or potential prey.

7 i whale evolution

ii Indian and African elephants

8 a allopatric evolution of reproductive isolation

b Climate change has resulted in warming of the Arctic Circle, allowing brown bears to expand their territory, overlapping polar bear habitats.

9 ecogeographic isolation

10 Neanderthal DNA may come from when modern humans (*Homo sapiens*) colonised the Neanderthal habitat and mated with them.

Unit 4 Practice assessment

RESEARCH INVESTIGATION

Student answers will vary depending on the research question and resources selected.

A sample research question:

'What evidence supports the "sixth mass extinction"? '

Resources should include information on when species started to decline, what events correlate with species declines, what the current statistics of species loss are, etc.